Praise for *Legacy in the Making*

"The foundation of a lasting business is meaning—a purpose bigger than profits or stock prices. This compelling, fascinating book will show you why, then help you discover the meaning that will guide your enduring business success."

Kevin Ashton, author, *How to Fly a Horse*, coined the term "Internet of Things"

"We live in an age where the way brands succeed is changing dramatically. We are moving away from a time when brands used to lead through command and control, by telling us what to buy, and toward one where they lead via sharing and influence, by inviting us in to help author their story. *Legacy in the Making* has it right. To achieve more than just fleeting success, to thrive long term in a short-term world, leaders need to not only write their brand's history every day, but also to coauthor it with those who share their ambition."

Jonah Berger, Wharton professor and bestselling author, *Contagious* and *Invisible Influence*

"The concept of legacy often feels like a 'looking backward calculation of what you've done.' This book flips that idea on its head, making legacy a daily and ongoing imperative. A modern legacy is a responsibility that takes time, care, and attention, attention, attention. This book will help many brands, old and new, chart their legacy path."

Caley Cantrell, strategy chair, Virginia Commonwealth University Brandcenter

"At the fundamental level, making a difference and having a social, positive impact in the typical business construct is hard. Corporate leaders must realize it's not about them, quarterly earnings, or profits. Leaving a legacy is long term. It's meaningfully focusing on generations beyond. To have a sound, sustainable, healthy business and to care for humanity, people, progress, and the planet, can only be achieved if your intentions are aligned with the true north of your values and principles. *Legacy in the Making* beautifully explores the important crossroads businesses face and, with story and heart, it aligns passion and purpose to amplify the power of business to lead, to be revolutionary, and to be a profound change agent for us all."

Christopher Gavigan, cofounder and chief purpose officer, The Honest Company, bestselling author, *Healthy Child Healthy World*

"Perhaps the notion of an enduring legacy can be summed up in the immortal words of the great disruptor Iggy Pop: 'I did my best. Now you do the rest.' What an amazing twit-obit! Mark Miller and Lucas Conley have captured the essence and DNA of true disruptors whose sole goal is to try to make the world a better place and then hand off to the next generation. This was the crucible in which the Tribeca Film Festival was forged after 9/11. It's an ideal this book celebrates in many rich and unconventional dimensions. *Legacy in the Making* is about leaders who aren't just capitalizing on trends, but who are making meaningful contributions we can all benefit from. It's not for the ones seeking 15 minutes of fame, but for the modern legacy-makers working to create change that lasts."

Craig Hatkoff, cofounder, Tribeca Film Festival

"I've long been inspired by those leaders who aim to make an indelible mark on the world. Not the ones just looking to make a quick buck, but the ones looking to make a lasting difference. In turn, I find myself drawn to the stories in *Legacy in the Making* for their ability to reveal more than just business successes, but also personal successes: the triumph of leaders who, despite the odds, continue to work to achieve something so important that they devote their lives to making it possible."

Hervé Humler, founding member and chairman emeritus, The Ritz-Carlton Hotel Company

"As leaders, we have all been given a wonderful gift, in that we live in fascinating times. In response to that gift, we now have the opportunity to make a beneficial, meaningful, and long-lasting impact. The case studies in *Legacy in the Making* provide me with an inspirational jolt of energy. The questions the authors raise are thought-provoking and encourage me to look at challenges differently. And the life stories in each chapter give me added confidence that a long-term vision, a laser-like focus on the needs and desires of others, and the strength of one's character will result in creating that meaningful impact. For an organization creating 'must-see' sporting events, this is definitely a 'must-read' book for all our people."

Christopher K. Kay, CEO and president, New York Racing Association, operator of Belmont Park and the Belmont Stakes

"This book is full of the kinds of lessons I have tried to explain to songwriters as well as aspiring small business owners—especially those seeking to emulate what I did at The Bluebird Cafe. Collected here, they act as a wonderful inspiration and guide for entrepreneurs. The authors have it right from the start: It's not about creating a business to make money, it's about creating a business that makes a difference. Once you do that, the money will follow."

Amy Kurland, founder, The Bluebird Cafe, Frances Williams Preston Mentor Award recipient, Source Nashville Hall of Fame honoree

"Legacy in the Making is that rare and insightful business book that reveals how the smartest brands author their legacies each day to drive growth, relevance, and impact. If you're a brand leader or marketer, grab this book. Better yet, share it with your entire company. "

Simon Mainwaring, founder and CEO, We First Inc., *New York Times* bestselling author, *We First*

"In a transient world preoccupied by 'likes' and advertising 'impressions,' people often confuse short-term success with purposeful significance. *Legacy in the Making* is a masterful, comprehensive, and thoughtful book that will steward you to achieve relevant, prosperous, and enduring brand strength. Mark Miller and Lucas Conley weave extensive research with practical real-world brand building skills into an engaging and thoughtful roadmap for activating a dynamic brand legacy. If you care about the impact of your brand stewardship, there is no better book for you."

Joseph Michelli, Ph.D., CCXP, *New York Times* #1 bestselling author, *The Starbucks Experience, Driven to Delight, The Zappos Experience*, and *The New Gold Standard*

"*Legacy in the Making* is a wonderfully refreshing oasis of long-term thinking in a vast contemporary desert of pernicious short-termism. Miller and Conley have given the thirsty among us a place to stay awhile, drink deep, and renew. An important and richly stimulating counterpoint to the powerful quarter-by-quarter undertow we all feel—and too often succumb to—in the business world around us."

Adam Morgan, founder, eatbigfish, international bestselling author, *Eating the Big Fish*, coauthor of *A Beautiful Constraint*

"*Legacy in the Making* is a powerful book that will enable entrepreneurs and executives alike to learn the trade secrets toward building a lasting, impactful brand and mission. This book is a true testament to the authors' and their networks' vast experience in founding and building companies that they are generously sharing with readers worldwide."

Tiffany Pham, founder and CEO, Mogul

"Do you want to thrive as a business? Then read *Legacy in the Making* to go beyond the short-term thinking that drags enterprises down into the muck of mediocrity. As authors Mark Miller and Lucas Conley make clear, it is a modern take on legacy that connects the past to the future. Modern legacy grows with each passing moment, every decision you make, every path you tread. So follow the prescriptions here to build your legacy the right way."

B. Joseph Pine II, coauthor, *The Experience Economy* and *Authenticity*

"A must-read to inspire and educate about what it means to be an effective leader and change-maker in today's ever-changing world."

Reshma Saujani, founder and CEO, Girls Who Code, *New York Times* bestselling author, *Girls Who Code* and *Women Who Don't Wait in Line*

"With *Legacy in the Making*, Mark Miller and Lucas Conley have given a name to the mindset that distinguishes enduring organizations from the ordinary. Many of the creative thinkers, undaunted do-ers, and selfless leaders profiled in this remarkable book are well known to us at *Fast Company* and *Inc.*, but I found myself inspired anew by hearing their stories in the framework of Mark's and Lucas's persuasive analysis. If it's your personal ambition to build a culture, a mission, an enterprise—a *brand*—that endures in this short-term-besotted business world, *Legacy in the Making* is your blueprint."

Eric Schurenberg, CEO of Mansueto Ventures, publisher of *Fast Company* and *Inc.* magazines

"Advertising and marketing have never been more difficult. With so much information, content, and media vying for our attention, company leaders—and the brands they represent—are looking for new strategies, almost daily. With the latest "real-time" data come new real-time strategic twists and turns for brands. Quick fixes are the order of the day, and the disease of short-termism is more rampant than ever. That's why Mark Miller and Lucas Conley's *Legacy in the Making* is so important. It is the perfect book for right now. It reminds business leaders, marketers, advertising agencies, and consultants that their primary goal should be to build lasting brands. In a short-term world, long-term thinking is the key to success."

Brian Sheehan, professor of advertising, S.I. Newhouse School of Public Communications, Syracuse University, author, *Loveworks*

"Legacy is so often misunderstood. Too many leaders treat the past as sacrosanct. Thinking that they are somehow abandoning the legacy if they change how things are done today. Legacy is not a museum. No leader should ever put their organization in formaldehyde. *Legacy in the Making* makes the case that legacy is about impact. It's about the future. This book is a must-read for anyone who wants their work to last beyond their lifetime."

Simon Sinek, optimist and *New York Times* bestselling author, *Start with Why* and *Leaders Eat Last*

"In a business world of rampant 'short-termism,' *Legacy in the Making* is an inspiring, practical, story-rich guidebook to help you grow your brand—in the short and long term—while achieving your own personal ambition. If Miller and Conley's energetic book does not compel you to create your modern legacy, I am not sure what will."

Jim Stengel, former global marketing officer, Procter & Gamble, author, *Unleashing the Innovators* and *Grow*

"I like to say that the only thing better than a good story is a good story that's true. *Legacy in the Making* explores good, truthful stories about the ways people and their companies are contributing to their legacies in the making every day. You will learn how one good decision leads to another, and how, when faced with the same forks in their road that others have encountered, these leaders chose a direction that built something long-lasting, learning as they went until it became second nature. The variety of industries covered in these pages proves that the right directions are chosen by leaders one decision at a time, no matter what business they're in, and that every business has the same opportunities to build something extraordinary."

Bob Taylor, cofounder and president, Taylor Guitars

"Yes, 13-year-olds read books about business and brand building. Well, maybe 13-year-olds like me and business books like this one. When I founded my company at the age of four, I wasn't thinking about big business. I was just focused on a big idea to make the world a better place for bees and for us. That's made all the difference for me and my brand. I discovered while reading this book that I'm in good company, too. Big ideas and even bigger change can come from anywhere, including you."

Mikaila Ulmer, founder and CEO, Me & the Bees Lemonade and the Healthy Hive Foundation, U.S. National Park Service Youth Ambassador, Eleanor Roosevelt Val-Kill Medal recipient

"We live in an age of tough questions, where answers matter more than ever. What do you stand for—just because it's right? What won't you stand for—just because it's wrong? Who do you stand with—just because that's who you are? This book will make you ask these and other fundamental questions. How you answer them will not only determine your brand in business, it will determine your identity in life."

Alan Webber, cofounder, *Fast Company* magazine

Legacy in the Making

*Building a Long-Term Brand
to Stand Out in a Short-Term World*

MARK MILLER **LUCAS CONLEY**

Founder of The Legacy Lab
and Chief Strategy Officer at Team One

Author of *Obsessive Branding Disorder*
and Coauthor of *The Method Method*

FOREWORD BY YVON CHOUINARD, FOUNDER OF PATAGONIA

New York   Chicago   San Francisco   Athens   London
Madrid   Mexico City   Milan   New Delhi
Singapore   Sydney   Toronto

1 2 3 4 5 6 7 8 9   LWI   23 22 21 20 19 18

ISBN   978-1-260-11756-1
MHID   1-260-11756-1

e-ISBN   978-1-260-11757-8
e-MHID   1-260-11757-X

Cover Design: Sawdust and Sophia Arriola-Gibson
Book Design: Adrienne Ford

McGraw-Hill Education books are available at special quantity discounts to use as premiums and sales promotions or for use in corporate training programs. To contact a representative, please visit the Contact Us pages at www.mhprofessional.com.

Library of Congress Cataloging-in-Publication Data

Names: Miller, Mark - author. | Conley, Lucas, author.
Title: Legacy in the making : building a long-term brand to stand out in a
    short-term world / Mark Miller and Lucas Conley.
Description: New York : McGraw-Hill, [2018] | Includes index.
Identifiers: LCCN 2017056194| ISBN 9781260117561 | ISBN
    1260117561
Subjects: LCSH: Branding (Marketing)
Classification: LCC HF5415.1255 .M5475 2018 | DDC 658.4--dc23 LC record available at
https://lccn.loc.gov/2017056194

For all those who believe that
the greatest legacies are forever
works in progress.

CONTENTS

Foreword

BY YVON CHOUINARD, FOUNDER OF PATAGONIA

My Personal Ambition

In April 2017, the authors of this book visited me at Patagonia's headquarters, in Ventura, California, to talk about the legacy I'm building as the founder of Patagonia. We talked about a lot of things, some of which I'd never spoken about before. Afterward, when they asked me if I'd share some of those insights and stories in the foreword to their book *Legacy in the Making*, I made it clear: I never wanted to be a conventional businessman. I liked climbing rocks, not corporate ladders.

"Exactly," they responded. "That's why we asked you."

It's true. I never set out to be a businessman. Over the years, I've learned a lot about business with Chouinard Equipment and Patagonia, the two outdoor outfitters I founded. But I'm a creature of the 1960s. I never liked authority. I was a rock climber. Back when I started climbing at the age of 19, the gear was poor quality. The pitons— the metal spikes you drive into cracks— were made of soft iron and were designed to be used once and left in place. The attitude back then was about dominating the mountains, conquering them and leaving all your gear behind to make it easier for the next party. I didn't share that attitude. I had a different ambition.

I wanted to climb without leaving a trace so that the next party and every party after that could experience the climb as I had— in its natural state. To do that, I needed a new kind of piton that you could remove and reuse over and over as you ascended. Since nothing like that existed at the time,

> Being on the cutting edge meant that we were not following the market. We weren't waiting for customers to tell us what to make.

I decided to design it myself. I bought an old coal-fired forge from a junkyard, built a small shop in my parents' backyard, taught myself how to blacksmith, and began making my own high-quality reusable pitons. They were the first of their kind, designed for a new style of climbing. I called my fledgling company Chouinard Equipment.

Initially, I was just a craftsman making climbing gear for myself and my friends. But I happened to be pretty good at it, and pretty soon I was selling gear to friends of friends out of the back of my car (whenever I wasn't surfing or climbing, that is). That evolved into making better crampons—the metal spikes on climbing boots—and better ice axes. With climbing, the better the tool, the better your chance of coming home in one piece. The quality of the materials and design—how the tool actually functioned in the field—was everything. People noticed, and by 1970 Chouinard Equipment had become the largest supplier of climbing equipment in the United States.

At that time, we were on the cutting edge of climbing. Some of the climbs we were doing in Yosemite National Park were harder than any rock climbs ever done in the world. Being on the cutting edge meant that we were not following the market. We weren't waiting for customers to tell us what to make. For example, when I started coming out with new tools for ice climbing, people had no idea how to use them, and so I began writing a book about it. The Austrians and Germans had different techniques than the French and the Scottish. I ran around the world and studied all the different techniques so that I could bring everything together in one unified method.

> Before we designed any new piece of clothing—whether it was an alpine jacket, a pair of socks, or a bikini—we always started by asking about function. What problem were we trying to solve?

In 1970, on my way home from climbing in Scotland, I bought a rugby shirt—a blue one with yellow and red stripes. Functionally, I thought it would be a great climbing shirt. It had a tough collar so that the gear slings wouldn't cut your neck and rubber buttons that wouldn't rip off. At that time, American sportswear was basically gray sweatpants and sweatshirts. That was it. There was no colored sportswear for men. Yet all of a sudden, here I was, wearing this really colorful shirt, and people were saying, "Wow, where'd you get that?" That was when we decided to start selling our own.

Our colors got pretty outrageous, but they also served a function. When you spend days suspended on a "big wall" climb or weeks stormbound in a tent, it's tough on your psyche. You want colorful clothes just for your own mental health.

We sold a lot of those rugby shirts. By 1973, we had launched a new brand, Patagonia, to focus on our growing clothing business. Unlike Chouinard Equipment (which we eventually sold to a group of employees who launched a brand called Black Diamond), we knew nothing about the established clothing industry when we started Patagonia. Zero. Conventional fashion designers take a mannequin, wrap cloth around it, pin it here and there, and create a dress. But our background was in designing lifesaving climbing gear, not fashion, and so we looked at clothes as tools.

Before we designed any new piece of clothing—whether it was an alpine jacket, a pair of socks, or a bikini—we always started by asking about function. What problem were we trying to solve? How would the product be *used*, not just worn? Which features would it need, and which would it

> Complexity is easy. The world is full of complex, disposable junk. Simplifying things, though—designing quality tools that last—now, that's hard.

not need? It's like Antoine de Saint-Exupéry said: "A designer knows he has achieved perfection not when there is nothing left to add, but when there is nothing left to take away." In retrospect, I think that is our biggest contribution to the clothing business: treating clothes as tools and applying the principles of industrial design.

When you approach products as tools that serve a function, it forces you to pare things down to their essence. Just look around. Complexity is easy. The world is full of complex, disposable junk. Simplifying things, though—designing quality tools that last—now, that's hard.

More than 60 years after I forged that first removable piton, we still approach everything we make just as I did in the beginning—as a simple, functional tool. The best tool for whatever your ambition is. As my ambition was to make better gear for the things I loved to do, my companies were the tools I used to achieve that ambition. But as your ambitions evolve, as mine would before long, so must your tools.

_____

Finding Our Way Back to the Real Patagonia

As the years have passed and Patagonia has grown, so have the brand's responsibilities. These days, we behave as if we want to be in business a hundred years from now. This is reflected in our mission statement: "Make the best product, cause no unnecessary harm, and use business to inspire and implement solutions to the environmental crisis." The mission statement is a tool, too. Like a compass, its function is to orient our brand culture and keep it moving in the right direction. But Patagonia didn't always work this way.

> I've always believed in making decisions by consensus as opposed to compromise.

In the early years, I ran the business like every other company. Just running it for the sake of getting larger and larger, doing everything that normal companies do. By the 1980s, we were taking off: opening new dealers, developing our own retail stores, and growing about 50 percent a year. You can't grow like that for very long before you end up in financial trouble. It's just impossible.

In 1990, the American economy went into recession. After years of growing just for the sake of growing, our sales suddenly hit a wall. The banks got into financial trouble,

and so did we. We couldn't borrow enough money to cover inventory, and we nearly lost the business. For the first time in our history, we had to lay people off—20 percent of our entire staff. Those people were like family, and the impact on our brand culture was a wake-up call. After we had been preoccupied with growth for years, our brand was adrift. Not only did we have to reassess our growth plans, we had to reassess who we were and who we wanted to be.

That was when I took our key managers— about 10 or 12 of us—and we all went down to Argentina, to the real Patagonia. We hiked around, sat down, and asked ourselves why we were in business and what we expected to get out of this. We asked each person why he or she was working for us. Though my ambition had always been to build the best tools, it was during this trip that we discussed our values:

- *Make the highest-quality products.*
- *Consider the environmental impact of everything we do.*
- *Engage and support our communities.*
- *Contribute a portion of our sales to philanthropy.*

No one said a word about profit.

Once we had collected everyone's thoughts, we established our brand values by consensus. I've always believed in making decisions by consensus as opposed to compromise. Compromise is what the government does. Compromise never solves a problem. Compromise leaves both sides feeling cheated. Consensus is how Native American tribes historically made decisions, and it was the chief's job to build consensus. That's been my role: to set the general direction we're going in and to get our employees to buy in.

After we got back from our trip to Patagonia, I started leading weeklong seminars to teach our employees about the values that would guide our brand culture moving forward. I wanted everyone to be empowered to make day-to-day decisions that were based on those values rather than always waiting for instructions from the boss. Years later, in 2005, I published everything—my ambition, our history, our growth crisis, our values—in *Let My People Go Surfing: The Education of a Reluctant Businessman*. Like those recyclable pitons, I didn't publish the book to get rich. I did it because as a reluctant businessman, I had learned an important lesson about business: Regardless of what you sell, your business itself—including your culture and your values—is your product. If we could inspire more values-based businesses, our society and environment would be a lot better off.

> Fiction is so much more difficult to write than nonfiction.

Let My People Go Surfing is still selling all over the world. They teach it in high schools, and it's been printed in 9 or 10 languages— all because people see the Patagonia brand as a different model.

The book you are holding now, *Legacy in the Making*, is proof that we're not alone in our beliefs. Brands with long-term ambitions and strong values-driven cultures are increasingly demonstrating that profits and purpose aren't mutually exclusive.

Lasting Brands Move People, Not Just Goods

I've always been an advocate for social and environmental causes, but I don't like being on the front lines. I get too frustrated. Instead, I've learned how to use business to effect change. We follow our beliefs, our customers follow us, and positive change tends to follow that. People who believe in what we're doing gravitate to our message. They become our advocates. That's why our marketing philosophy is so simple: We tell people who we are and what we do. That's it. Fiction is so much more difficult to write than nonfiction.

For us, marketing isn't about moving goods. It's about moving people. For example, in 2011 we ran a print ad on Black Friday that said, "Don't buy this jacket." We sold so many of those jackets! That wasn't the intent. The intent was to encourage people to reflect on what they buy and to buy only what they need. The best thing you can do for the environment as far as clothing goes is to buy the very best quality, use it as long as possible, and keep it out of the landfill. Repair it. Reuse it. Recycle it.

> At the end of the year, we measure success by how much good we've done and by what impact we're having on society, not by profit.

That Black Friday campaign forced us to make a pact with our customers: If you buy one of our jackets, we'll repair it forever. If you outgrow it or stop using it, we'll help you sell it to somebody else. Eventually we'll take it back and melt it down into more jackets. It forced us to build the largest garment repair facility in North America. In fact, we have a truck that goes around to colleges and teaches kids how to sew buttons on. We'll repair any of their clothes, not just ours. We practice business this way because our customers are our loyal sales force, and they pay far more attention to good deeds than to lofty words.

For our 2016 Black Friday campaign, we decided to give all the revenue away to environmental causes. Not just the profits. All of our revenue that day. As a result, our sales quadrupled, from $2.5 million the previous year to over $10 million for Black Friday 2016. We gave away all $10 million—in addition to the $9 million contribution we made that same year in line with our annual commitment to contribute 1 percent of our sales to charity.[1] Philanthropic campaigns like this don't cut into our sales. In fact, 60 percent of our customers from these campaigns are new. Just think about how much it costs most companies to get new customers. The social media aspect of this campaign cost us nothing. We let the word out, and in turn, our customers helped spread the word for us.

At the end of the year, we measure success by how much good we've done and what impact we're having on society, not by profit. Honestly, if you ask me how much money we've made in the last year, I would have to look it up. I know that we are extremely profitable. I also believe in karma. Karma and profits coexist here because every time we've made a decision in service of doing good, our customers have noticed. And when our customers get behind us, more good things follow.

Write Your Own Rules, Don't Master Someone Else's

I know it's unorthodox to be guided by both karma and profits, but that's just one of many ways we break the rules of business these days. I think of Patagonia less as a conventional brand selling products than as an experiment, an evolving means of using business to solve social problems.

If you look around and see who's working here, we all have degrees in subjects such as

> When you chase short-term profits, you either keep doing what you already know will work or copy what someone else is doing. We don't do that.

anthropology, zoology, and English. Only a few of us actually have degrees in business. We're all learning how to run a business by asking lots of questions and approaching things as beginners. We're successful because we have the confidence to write our own rules rather than master someone else's.

Maybe that's why we're comfortable being a guinea pig and trying new things. We're making healthy food and producing films about society's impact on the natural world. We're even thinking about starting an immersive nature school for kids. As uncon-

ventional as these programs may sound, all of them are firmly rooted in our ambitions and values. Ultimately, the next generation won't care about nature if they don't think they're part of it. So while our values haven't changed, the way we choose to express those values to new generations of customers is always evolving.

At Patagonia, it's not that we're just looking for ways to stand out for the sake of standing out. Like the leaders profiled in this book, we behave differently because our ambitions are different. We also measure success differently—on the basis of long-term contributions, not short-term profits. When you chase short-term profits, you either keep doing what you already know will work or copy what someone else is doing. We don't do that. When we stand out, it's because we've found a new way to express our long-term ambitions.

In the mid-1990s, for example, we took a stand against chemically intensive cotton and began making all of our clothes with organic cotton. It was a challenge, and a lot of our manufacturing partners walked away from us, but we learned by doing and ultimately developed our own private cotton supply chain. Most people aren't willing to jump right in like that. But that's the way I like to deal with everything. Most people want to figure things out to the nth degree before they ever take a step. In the end, they won't even take that step because it feels too unfamiliar. Not me. I immediately jump in and see how it feels. That's how I know we're on the cutting edge—when we step outside conventions and lead the market rather than follow it. This approach takes vision and perseverance, but it keeps us in a category of our own. As the saying goes, "First they ignore you, then they ridicule you, then they fight you, and then you win."

I was on a panel during the recent recession, and it was all surf industry CEOs and people like that. We all talked about our businesses, and I talked about how much effort we put into cleaning up our supply chain and trying not to cause unnecessary harm. One of the CEOs from one of the largest surf companies told me his company had been making a few organic cotton ball caps and T-shirts before the recession but had cut back when the economy slowed down.

I said, "How are your sales?"

He said, "Well, we're down about 25 percent." Patagonia was up 30 percent. That company ultimately filed for bankruptcy. Today the surf industry is on the rocks, but we're doing great because we're riding our own wave.

The Secret to Lasting Is to Keep Playing Your Own Game

I've been in business for over 60 years. I've survived bad times. I've thrived in good times. I believe the secret to lasting is never sitting still.

Some people see change as a threat. They hate it. I thrive on it, as does every ecosystem as well as every business that cares about its legacy in the making. I'm not talking about change for the sake of change. I'm talking about evolving and adapting as if you intend on being here a hundred years from now; it's about never losing sight of where you came from or what inspired you in the first place.

Although we try to run Patagonia as if it's going to be here a hundred years from now, I tell my employees that doesn't mean we have a hundred years to get there. Continuous change requires a sense of urgency. That's why my job these days is to combat complacency and instigate change. There's a falconry term—*yarak*—that means superalert, hungry, and ready to hunt. Along with our other leaders, one of my responsibilities is to keep the company in *yarak*.

The best way I keep us from sitting still is by using what I've learned to educate and inspire the next generation of leaders, which includes the following:

- *Have an ambition to develop better tools.*
- *Growth can be toxic, though culture can be a tonic.*
- *Move people, not just products.*
- *Be distinct in everything we do.*
- *Evolve and change to remain unique.*
- *Long-term values can guide quick decision-making every day.*

As the authors of this book say, "The making of a legacy is personal, behavioral, influential, unconventional, and perpetual." These lessons don't expire, and through education they can transcend generations. So I share my story—as I have here—to pass my legacy forward for others to carry on.

The authors of this book talk about the importance of long-term thinking in a short-term world. It's true, though it's never easy. Conventional business will fight you every step of the way. Long-term investments in programs such as our brand's employee childcare center and our pollution standards always look negative on our financial ledger. But because we think long-term, we know we have responsibilities beyond our conventional bottom line. So do you. So does every great brand leader.

If you're reading this book, you may already believe that your culture is your product, not what you sell. You may also believe, like me, that companies shouldn't exist simply to be sold for a profit and broken apart. Of course, this isn't how conventional business works. Conventional business treats companies like fatted calves to be auctioned to the highest bidder in the shortest amount of time. It's the American way. It starts when we're young, when they say, "Okay, kids, line up on the starting line and let's see who can run the fastest! Now line up over here, kids, and let's see who can jump the highest!" That way of thinking produces one superhero and a bunch of losers. But, I wanted to do something different. I always have.

Growing up, I was as good as anybody at baseball and football and other sports. But when it came time to line up and perform for a crowd, I couldn't do it. So I've been a climber, a kayaker, a falconer, a Telemark skier, a spear fisherman—all noncompetitive sports. All individual pursuits where your only competition is how high you set your personal ambitions.

That's my advice to you as you build your legacy in the making: Invent your own game. Ask yourself what you hope to get out of this life, let that enduring ambition guide you, and if the right tools don't exist to accomplish it, design your own tools. Be the only person who does what you do the way you do it. That way, you will always be the winner.

— **Yvon Chouinard**
Founder of Patagonia

Yvon Chouinard ascending a rock wall near Telluride, Colorado, in 1981. "I had a different ambition," says Patagonia's founder. "I wanted to climb without leaving a trace."

Denver Post/*Getty Images*

The End of Legacy as We Know It

THE STORY OF Patagonia, as shared in the Foreword, is an inspiring example of the power of long-term personal ambition in a short-term world. But for every Patagonia, there are many more cautionary tales, such as Blockbuster, Borders, and Kodak. Once synonymous with the videos, books, and film they sold, these three iconic brands all filed for Chapter 11 bankruptcy protection in the space of just 16 months between 2010 and 2012.[1] Their falls from grace sent chills through global markets and popular culture. At its height, each commanded an industry and appeared to control its own destiny, employing tens of thousands of people around the world and generating billions in annual revenue. Consumers loved them. Competitors feared them. It once seemed impossible to imagine the world without them. Today, however, less than a decade later, one of these brands no longer exists, another is near defunct, and the third is still hoping for, but has not yet realized, its second life.[2]

There are brands that rest on their laurels, and there are brands that add a page to their story every day. Once Blockbuster, Borders, and Kodak stopped doing the latter, they became the former—and they began to die. Since each brand filed for bankruptcy protection, countless articles and books have autopsied their decline in exhausting detail, but the synopsis for all three is the same: Each is the story of a once-famous brand that stayed stuck in the past instead of continually bringing the world forward.

> *Those who repeat the past are essentially playing it safe.*

As a strategist and a journalist, respectively, authors Mark Miller and Lucas Conley—hereafter *we*—have spent our entire careers telling other people's stories. Some leaders and brands come to us fully aware of the message they want to share. Others ask us to translate their messages for them. Few expect their stories to end, but too many, such as Blockbuster, Borders, and Kodak, lose their way.

In today's short-term economy, long-term success stories are increasingly hard to find. Twenty percent of all U.S. businesses fail within the first year. Nearly half are gone by the five-year mark. Only one out of three survives to celebrate its 10-year anniversary.[3] Even among the biggest, most recognized brands, long-term survival is increasingly rare. In the 1920s, the average life span of a company listed on the Standard & Poor's 500—a list of the top 500 publicly traded companies in the world—was 67 years.[4] Today, it's just 15 years.[5] That means that the playground equipment at your local park now outlasts many of the world's biggest companies.[6]

Short-termism isn't limited to brands; it also affects the people who work for and lead them. According to the U.S. Bureau of Labor Statistics, average employee tenure numbers are declining, depleting corporate ranks of consistency and culture. Between 2014 and 2016 (the most recent period for which data was published), median job tenure in the United States dropped 11.5 percent to 4.2 years.[7] The decline was even steeper for chief marketing officers at major U.S. brands: Their tenure shrank by six months—to just 3.5 years—during that same period.[8] With corporate and career life spans locked in a downward spiral, it's no wonder only a third of people consider themselves engaged at work.[9]

Caught in this short-term spin cycle, careers and brands that last are becoming a scarce resource. The antidote to this outbreak—as Yvon Chouinard demonstrates at Patagonia—is to build your brand through the lens of legacy. Not the old-world legacy that's bequeathed from the past. We're talking about a new kind of legacy that simultaneously encompasses what was and what will be. Whether yours is a young brand aiming to endure or an established one seeking to remain vital for generations to come, this book marks a turning point in the way brands are built.

This is the end of legacy as we know it.

The Call for a New Kind of Legacy

We're all familiar with the traditional meaning of legacy, as evidenced by the steady churn of autobiographies, bequests, commemorations, and dedications we are forever leaving in our collective cultural wake. We see it in every leader who seeks to "cement" his or her legacy as if it were something set in stone and left behind on a museum pedestal to gather dust. This is the problem with traditional legacy. It's backward-looking. Stuck in the past. An anchor. Static.

In contrast, our lives are anything but static; they evolve fluidly on a continuum. Just as we reflect on our past milestones for inspiration and guidance, we draw motivation from everything we still hope to accomplish. Inspired by long-term personal ambition, each of us is capable of continually crafting his or her legacy in the here and now by adding to it every day. Traditional legacy is no longer suited for today's short-term economy. Traditional legacy is about telling the same old story. Today's circumstances call for a dynamic way of looking at brand building that fosters nimble and resilient brands that are perpetually in the making—neither forgetting the past nor getting stuck in it—as the world constantly changes around them.

> *Those who revile the past see it as an obstacle to making their mark now.*

Seeking to better understand how companies inherit, create, and pass along their living stories, Miller established The Legacy Lab at Team One in 2012.[10] Working with a group of leading strategists and experts from disciplines such as cultural anthropology, data analytics, and semiotics, we started by researching pioneering brands. We looked at established brands and upstarts alike. No company was too small, too big, too young, or too old. Our focus was on the story behind those companies: What kind of legacy were they building? How were they enduring and thriving?

Through this research, we began conducting global surveys of brand builders everywhere, gradually formalizing the way we collected, processed, and analyzed the feedback. Then we reached out to leaders at some of the world's best-known and most innovative companies to request in-depth interviews. We suspected that they would have a lot to teach us about building brands to last, and they did, but what these leaders observed in the world around them was equally intriguing—and troubling.

First, the Trouble: The Short-Term Thinker's Blind Spot

Soon after we began conducting in-person interviews, we discovered an unnervingly pervasive flaw in the way many people think about building brands. Although the leaders we approached tended to describe their leg-acies as forward-looking ambitions—such as the desire to solve a problem, improve an industry, or protect and grow something meaningful—they consistently lamented that many of their peers fell into one of two nearsighted traps: The first is repeating the past. The second is reviling it.

Those who repeat the past are essentially playing it safe. They prefer to stick with what they know rather than change things and risk screwing up. After all, they reason, even if they fail, who could fault them for doing what always worked in the past? In the words of one Legacy Lab respondent, "No one wants to go down in history as the person who changed the formula for Coca-Cola."

Those who revile the past see it as an obstacle to making their mark now. Eager to validate themselves and highly conscious of how little time they have to demonstrate results in light of receding corporate life spans and employee tenures, they see themselves as change agents racing to capture attention before time is up.

As different as these methods appear, both approaches exhibit the same myopia. Both are shortsighted because they mismanage the past, either clinging to it too closely or rejecting it outright. In concert, these near-sighted flaws amount to a false dilemma, a black-and-white way of viewing the world that results in something we refer to as the short-term thinker's blind spot. The brands that play it safe do themselves a disservice. They may temporarily protect the status quo by anchoring themselves to the past, but they risk diminishing their relevance as the world continues to change around them. Meanwhile, the brands that look to make their mark quickly as change agents risk jettisoning their heritage and identity, leaving them rudderless and adrift in mercurial markets.

Propelled by myopic thinking, short-termism is taking a heavy toll on our culture and economy, sapping the souls of modern brands and the employees who fill their ranks, and even redefining our understanding of and appreciation for things that last and flourish—things with enduring legacy. We wondered: How are leaders at today's most ambitious brands avoiding this blind spot?

Now, the Intrigue: Five Transformations, One Mindset

Six years, 20 countries, and thousands of surveys and interviews later (and counting), The Legacy Lab has amassed an insightful body of knowledge on the dynamics of long-term brand building in a short-term world. More often than not, what we are finding is that the commercial success enjoyed by enduring brands is matched by an equally inspiring story of personal leadership and ambition. In this book, we have collected a number of these lasting success stories. All point to a new approach to brand building: a long-term, ambition-driven way of creating something of enduring worth and significance.

Modern legacy brands are not museums.

Legacy in the Making celebrates a dynamic form of brand building seen through the eyes of a select group of extraordinary men and women who are living out their ambitions in the age of now. Some are founders or cofounders of their own companies. Some—those we call refounders—lead businesses established by others. All are actively building enduring brands that are informed by the past, drawn by the future, and forged continually in the present. We define this active method of brand building as the making of modern legacy. Whereas traditional legacy is static, modern legacy can no more be cemented than time itself.

Embracing this active interpretation of legacy building—one in which your story never ends—involves continually reconciling past achievements and future goals while building your brand in the present. Traditional legacy brands, for example, are strictly caretakers of the past. In contrast, modern legacy builders are also the authors of a vital today and tomorrow. Rather than simply repeating history, they add to their stories every day, harnessing their long-term personal ambitions and inspiring others to carry

> *The best short-term strategy is a long-term one.*

their brands forward. Modern legacy brands are not museums. They're not left behind. The brand legacies you will find here are all *in the making*.

Guided by personal ambitions, the modern legacy builders in these pages respond quickly to new competitive challenges, unexpected crises, and evolving market conditions. Informed by long-term ambitions, these leaders are actually faster, better short-term decision makers than their nearsighted competitors. This insight led us to the counterintuitive thesis at the heart of this book: *The best short-term strategy is a long-term one.*

This isn't just a book of business tactics. It's a book about the profound transformations in business and brand building that we observed again and again throughout our research. Most important, it's a book about how you can take advantage of these brand-building transformations as you set out to achieve your own legacy in the making.

Modern legacy builders—leaders who envision their legacies in the making as opposed to something static or in the past tense—not only think and talk about their work differently, they are transforming the entire business landscape in distinct and powerful ways. The closer we looked during the course of our research, the more it became clear that these transformative perspectives were all part of one cohesive mindset—a dynamic, visionary worldview better suited to our rapidly evolving economy than the outdated strategies of nearsighted brands looking only to survive for the short term.

Whereas short-term thinkers focus solely on conventional measures of success such as profits, growth, capturing consumers, dominating categories, and achieving their 15 minutes of fame, modern legacy builders ask more of themselves and their brands,

leading to five far-reaching transformations in the way enduring brands are built in the modern age:

1. **From following institutional practices to leading with personal ambitions**

2. **From attitudinal posturing to behaving your beliefs**

3. **From commanding and controlling customers to influencing social movements**

4. **From obeying orthodox boundaries to pioneering unconventional solutions**

5. **From episodic innovation to perpetual adaptation**

Together, these five transformative perspectives on brand building constitute what we call the modern legacy mindset. Each chapter of this book is devoted to exploring one of these transformations and illustrating how modern legacy builders differ from their nearsighted peers.

Additionally, to bring the five transformations of the modern legacy mindset to life,

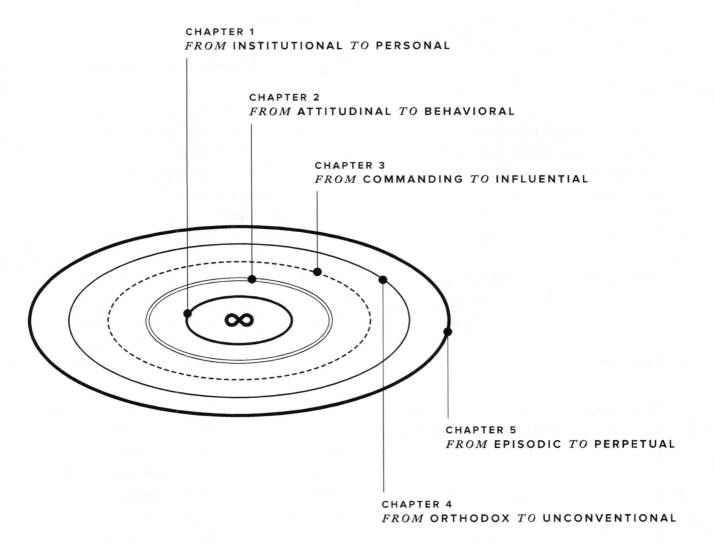

CHAPTER 1
FROM INSTITUTIONAL *TO* PERSONAL

CHAPTER 2
FROM ATTITUDINAL *TO* BEHAVIORAL

CHAPTER 3
FROM COMMANDING *TO* INFLUENTIAL

CHAPTER 5
FROM EPISODIC *TO* PERPETUAL

CHAPTER 4
FROM ORTHODOX *TO* UNCONVENTIONAL

Mapping the Modern Legacy Mindset

Each chapter in *Legacy in the Making* explores one of the five key ways modern legacy builders are transforming the world of work.

each chapter in *Legacy in the Making* includes the following elements:

- **Inspirations**

  Three stories, each with its own inspiring lesson, drawn from in-depth interviews with successful modern legacy leaders.

- **Applications**

  Provocative thoughts and questions about how to apply the lessons at hand to crafting your own modern legacy.

- **Summation**

  A summary of how the inspirations and applications covered in the chapter are transforming the world of work.

- **The Legacy Builder's Balance Sheet**

  Modern methods for qualitatively gauging the impact of difficult-to-measure concepts such as ambition, behavior, influence, originality, and perseverance.

Our Personal Ambition as Authors

Although there is no shortage of business books featuring fast-twitch solutions, books based on enduring personal ambitions are few and far between. After all, shilling one short-term answer is much easier than stoking countless lasting ambitions. But we're not here to give you all the answers; that isn't our goal. This book is intended to help you discover your own answer. Rather than a recipe, a formula, or a step-by-step solution, we offer you a mindset for achieving your own version of the remarkable. Rather than instructions, we offer you inspiration.

Over the next couple hundred pages, we will share stories of legacies in the making across brands of all ages and in all categories. By the time you have finished this book, our hope is that you not only will be able to tell the difference between nearsighted brands mired in short-term thinking and modern brand legacies guided by long-term ambition—but you will be inspired to begin building your own legacy in the making.

Rest assured, it will be difficult. If there were shortcuts to achieving professional success and personal fulfillment while creating lasting change, many more would be doing it. There would be no need for a book like this. Therefore, bring an appetite for risk, a willingness to fail, and the resolve to keep trying. Although this book offers guiding principles and useful tools, none of the leaders highlighted in these pages got where they are by checking off boxes. Instead, they are using the modern legacy mindset to build significant brands that will endure and thrive.

The time has never been better. The scarcity of people pursuing their long-term personal ambitions—as well as the ever-increasing, short-term distractions and incentives not to do this—presents a unique competitive opportunity for leaders with the modern legacy mindset.

When the economy crashes, nearsighted companies cut from all corners. But modern legacy builders do not compromise their ambitions. In fact, they rely on the principles of the modern legacy mindset to sustain them through recessions, competitive pressures, fickle sales trends, tight job markets, and any number of other unpredictable challenges. When the direction ahead is unclear, this mindset illuminates the way. As a result, the modern legacy builders profiled in the pages of this book are outperforming rivals, attracting and keeping the best talent, and changing the way others engage with their work and think about their own legacies in the making. Equipped with their insights, you too can harness your personal ambition to build a brand that lasts.

This is the end of legacy as we know it. This is the start of something new.

CHAPTER ONE

Take Leadership Personally

"[M]y goal was never to just create a company. A lot of people misinterpret that, as if I don't care about revenue or profit or any of those things. But what not being 'just a company' means to me is just that—building something that actually makes a really big change in the world."

MARK ZUCKERBERG

Cofounder, Chairman, and Chief Executive Officer, Facebook[1]

IN THE FALL OF 2007, Mark Zuckerberg turned down a $24 billion offer from Microsoft for his three-year-old social networking upstart, Facebook.[2] If he had taken the offer and handed over the reins, Zuckerberg, then just 23 years old, would have walked away with an estimated $4 billion.[3] What inspired the young college dropout to refuse such an enormous payout? An even larger personal ambition: Zuckerberg doesn't dream of collecting wealth, he dreams of connecting the world.

From his Harvard dormitory to Facebook's 430,000-square-foot headquarters in Silicon Valley, Zuckerberg's zeal for connection has guided every decision he has made.[4] Each step of the way, his devotion to his long-term personal ambition has distinguished him from conventional peers who play by the book. Though Microsoft reportedly made Zuckerberg various offers that would allow him to maintain some degree of control, none were satisfactory.[5] In 2009, after China, for political reasons, blocked its 1.3 billion citizens from using Facebook, Zuckerberg demonstrated his commitment to and appreciation for the Chinese nation and its people by learning Mandarin.[6] In 2015, he pledged to donate 99 percent of his wealth during his lifetime to promoting education, curing disease, and "connecting people and building strong communities."[7] Every acquisition along the way—whether it was the photo-sharing app Instagram or WhatsApp,

the world's largest messaging service—has been in service of better connecting the world. The results have been unprecedented.

About 10 years after Microsoft's $24 billion offer, Facebook's market value has topped $500 billion.[8] At last check, Zuckerberg was worth an estimated $72 billion, making him one of the richest people on the planet.[9] But nowhere is the success of Zuckerberg's personal ambition more obvious than in the expansion of Facebook's user base, which continues to grow by double digits each year.[10] In 2007, Facebook had 50 million users.[11] Today, that number is over 2 billion,[12] representing more than a quarter of the world's total population.[13]

It's hard to imagine Facebook having the same success if Zuckerberg had sold it to Microsoft years ago. Similarly, it's difficult to see Facebook's success having continued if Zuckerberg had allowed Wall Street to steer the brand solely in the interest of dividends and profit margins. Facebook is literally a half-trillion-dollar expression of Zuckerberg's desire to connect the world.

To this day, Zuckerberg remains personally invested in guiding his brand and accomplishing his long-term personal ambition. In light of this dedication to his ambition and his brand, Zuckerberg is emblematic of the first transformation in the modern legacy mindset: the shift from following institutional practices to leading with personal ambitions.

Transformation:

Nearsighted brand leaders buy in to management systems and institutional processes with the goal of following market trends.

Leaders with the modern legacy mindset invest in individuals who are seeking to make a meaningful contribution, beginning with their own long-term personal ambitions.

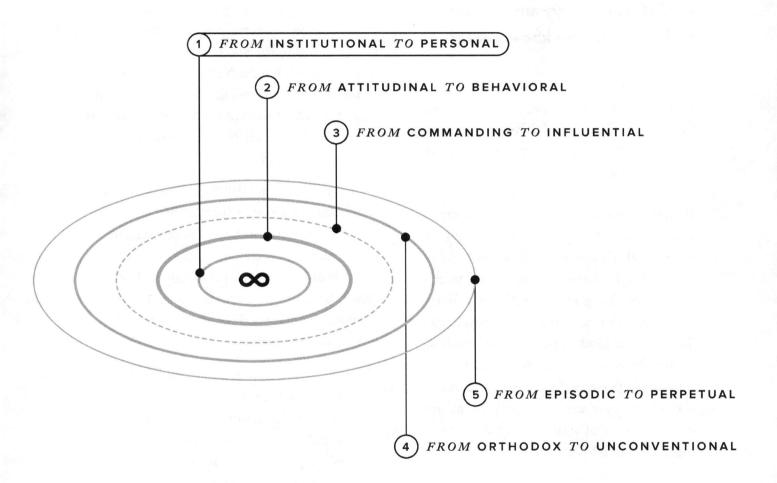

1 *FROM* INSTITUTIONAL *TO* PERSONAL

2 *FROM* ATTITUDINAL *TO* BEHAVIORAL

3 *FROM* COMMANDING *TO* INFLUENTIAL

5 *FROM* EPISODIC *TO* PERPETUAL

4 *FROM* ORTHODOX *TO* UNCONVENTIONAL

Every legacy in the making begins with a long-term personal ambition. Do you know yours?

In this chapter, we examine three modern legacy brands—the Tribeca Film Festival, Girls Who Code, and NYX Cosmetics— and the leaders who built those brands on their personal ambitions.

Before we begin, however, we should explain what we mean when we say modern legacy is personal. Of course, whatever you do for a living is "personal" because it's your occupation. *You* go to the office, *you* do the work, and it's *your* name on the paychecks. This isn't the kind of personal we're talking about. When we say "modern legacy building is personal," we mean that you should *take your work personally*. If you are not the author of your own legacy in the making, who is?

There will always be people who tell you not to bring your work home with you, to leave it at the office. We're not those people.

Modern legacies aren't just built between 9 and 5. They don't rest on weekends and holidays. Once you identify your personal ambition, your legacy in the making will follow you wherever you go. Epiphanies will arrive in the shower when pen and paper aren't handy. New ideas will spring up just as you turn out the lights and rest your head on the pillow. Modern legacy, as the musician Neil Young famously said of rust, never sleeps.

If you're familiar with the inspiring power of long-term personal ambition, you understand the transformative effect it can have on the way you lead through your work. The value of taking work personally is that you will try harder, stick with it longer, and bring more creativity and imagination to it than will anyone working just for a paycheck.

Ultimately, building a modern legacy is about more than accumulating material riches; it's also about cultivating an abundance of emotional richness.[14] When you pursue a personal ambition, the work itself is enjoyable, not just the success. In Zuckerberg's case, he has been willing to pass up billions of dollars, learn one of the most difficult languages on Earth, and even pledge 99 percent of his wealth to charity in service of his personal ambition.

In contrast, people motivated only by money generally fall into two camps: those who work just enough to pay their bills and those whose paycheck is never big enough. If this is you, it's time to break camp and begin taking things more personally. Consider that even the most "selfless" pursuits, such as those which involve helping others for little or no pay, are more lasting, impactful, and rewarding when we invest more of our "selves" in them.

What are your enduring personal ambitions? This may sound like that age-old question "What are you going to do with your life?" but don't get stuck or overwhelmed searching for a profound answer. As you'll see in the stories that follow, often there is no searching involved at all. Leaders with a modern legacy mindset encounter opportunities all around them. Most admit that they never sought out these ambitions; their ambitions found them. Some arise from personal or professional difficulty. Others appear during periods of transition, confusion, boredom, and even shock. For those of

us who are paying attention and taking our work personally, new ambitions have a way of making themselves heard.

In the case of Toni Ko, whose story appears later in this chapter, personal ambition called from the past. Reshma Saujani, another modern legacy builder featured in the pages that follow, stumbled upon her personal ambition in passing. All too commonly the deepest personal ambitions are inspired by injustice, suffering, or tragedy—problems that draw our best qualities out of us. This is the case in our first example, the story of the Tribeca Film Festival, as shared with us by cofounder Craig Hatkoff.

① Contribution Before Extraction

THE TRIBECA FILM FESTIVAL

Established 2002

② Opportunities Out of Obstacles

GIRLS WHO CODE

Established 2012

③ Lead, Don't Manage

NYX COSMETICS

Established 1999

IN THE FALL OF 2001, Robert De Niro, Jane Rosenthal, and Craig Hatkoff looked out the windows of their Tribeca office and saw a wasteland. Neighborhood streets, once swarming with brightly clad tourists and Wall Street power brokers in dark suits, were silent, empty, and sealed off by police barriers. The hustle and bustle of cabs, bike messengers, and delivery vans that normally clogged major arteries such as Canal Street and Broadway had been replaced by the grim shuffle of bulldozers, backhoes, dump trucks, and cranes making their way to and from Ground Zero—"the pile," as it came to be known to locals. A ghostly fine dust covered everything, lingering atop rows of unused parking meters, dark and vacant windowsills, and even the police barricades. Life in Lower Manhattan had come to a standstill.

It's difficult to overstate the profound impact 9/11 had on the people of Tribeca. Immediately north of the World Trade Center, this neighborhood of industrial buildings converted to residential lofts extends north roughly 17 blocks to Canal Street. The area, situated in the heart of Lower Manhattan, got its name from being the "*Tri*angle *Be*low

*Ca*nal Street." On the morning of the terrorist attacks, as the towers collapsed, thousands lost their lives and millions fled the city in panic. Mayor Rudolph Giuliani advised New Yorkers: "If you are south of Canal Street, get out. Walk slowly and carefully. If you can't figure what else to do, just walk north."

Giuliani's words seemed to echo through Tribeca's empty streets for months. Long after the physical debris was cleared, the psychological damage remained. Without customers, retailers, street vendors, bars, and restaurants were shuttered. And it wasn't just Tribeca. In a place that once felt like the center of the world, living and working in Lower Manhattan had become a matter of survival. As the days turned to weeks, desperation began to take hold.

"There was no one in Little Italy, Chinatown, or the financial district," Hatkoff recalls. "People realized if we didn't all do something, these restaurants would go out of business. How do you get people back to normalcy after a terrorist attack?"

Seeking to help before the damage became irreversible, De Niro, Rosenthal, and Hat-

koff began looking for a way to draw people back to the neighborhood they loved. It was ambitious, but bringing life back to the streets of Tribeca was a goal they all shared. Precisely how they were going to accomplish it was still up for discussion. Working with friends in the area, they came up with their first idea: "Dinner Downtown."

"We did the equivalent of an old-fashioned social media campaign," says Hatkoff. "We organized dinners where a person had to invite 10 more, and they in turn had to invite 10 more. We organized it to go to several dozen restaurants in the area."

The first Dinner Downtown event was a hit. Held shortly after 9/11, it drew some 600 people, including headline-grabbing guests such as Bill Clinton and Queen Noor of Jordan.

As one successful dinner event followed the next, the trio began thinking bigger. What if they could bring not just hundreds but thousands—perhaps even tens of thousands—of visitors to the neighborhood? What if they could not only revive Tribeca but give it something to rally around for

years to come? And what if they could do all of that by following their own personal passion—film (De Niro as an actor, Rosenthal as a producer, and Hatkoff as an entrepreneur and industry enthusiast)? Though De Niro and Rosenthal had discussed creating a film festival before, the idea had never made sense. Now, with their neighborhood in peril, the time was right.

"That was the germ of the idea," says Hatkoff. "The moment when we said this could work."

———————

Moments of inspiration like the one Hatkoff mentions above are some of our favorites at The Legacy Lab. Some call them *aha* moments. For Hatkoff and his fellow cofounders, it was the "germ of the idea." In each instance, the spark of inspiration is generated at the nexus of a personal ambition (in this case revitalizing a neighborhood) and a personal value (here the craft of filmmaking). This nexus is the foundation on which all modern legacies are built. Although we are all capable of iden-

DINNER DOWNTOWN! with ONE HUNDRED HEROES!!
(It's Family Night in Chinatown!!)

TO: Dinner Captains (please invite 5 other couples/families

FROM: Robert De Niro, Jane Rosenthal, Craig Hatkoff

RE: DINNER DOWNTOWN! Tuesday December 18th

Dear Friend:

Right after our first **DINNER DOWNTOWN!** we were asked by a group of firefighters if we would organize a special event where they could be the hosts to show their appreciation for everything New Yorkers have been doing for them and to help play a part in helping downtown. On Tuesday evening, December 18th, we will hold a special **DINNER DOWNTOWN!** honoring One Hundred Heroes (FDNY, NYPD EMS PAPD etc) and their families who will be **our co-hosts** at all the restaurants. This is a family event!! We will start with a short parade at 5:30 when our children and we can march down Mott St with our heroes (and the dragons of Chinatown).

As a Dinner Captain, we would like you to invite/organize a group of five families/couples.

On Wednesday November 7th, we launched the first **DINNER DOWNTOWN!** The goal was modest: we hoped to attract about a hundred of our friends to support the downtown restaurants. However, within 72 hours the ranks swelled to almost 600 people joining us for dinner at 27 downtown restaurants throughout Little Italy, Chinatown and Wall St. [You helped this event become a smashing success]. The event received enormous press coverage and, in turn, generated a huge general awareness and future interest in what started out as a little idea. The goal still remains simple: to help these restaurants stay in business by simply giving them our business.

We now ask you to help us again (or join us for the first time) **for DINNER DOWNTOWN!** for this special event- Family Night. Starting right after the first of the year **DINNER DOWNTOWN!** will become a regular weekly event. This will be the last opportunity in 2001. See you there!

Bob, Jane & Craig

DATE & TIME: Tuesday evening, December 18th
5:00 PM Everyone meets at 62 Mott Street (Chinese Benevolence Assoc.)
5:15 PM Press Conference
5:30 PM Mini-parade (with our Heroes and the Dragons of Chinatown)
6:00 PM Dinner begins

COST: Dutch treat ($30 per adult/ $15 per c
Please bring cash- many restaurants
cards

RSVP: by phone or by fax

SPECIAL CO-HOSTS: Each restaurant to be co-hosted by a
FDNY, PAPD, EMS etc

CORPORATE

> *"The world didn't need another film festival, but Tribeca did."*

tifying our ambitions and values, surprisingly few of us actually harness them. In the end, many people confess that work is a means to an end rather than an end within itself.

Early on, our research identified a clear distinction in the way modern legacy builders think about meaning and ambition in their work. People with a long-term personal ambition don't generally start out aiming just to get rich, grow market share, or become famous—goals based on a desire to *extract* something from the world. They start from the other end of the philosophical spectrum, asking questions such as "What problem can I solve?" and "What can I offer that no one else can?"— objectives inspired by a desire to *contribute*.

Perhaps counterintuitively, starting from a contributory mindset—as De Niro, Rosenthal, and Hatkoff did—gives rise to a host of opportunities and competitive advantages. Consider that there is never a shortage of people looking to get rich and that most people who set out to do that tend to think just like everyone else trying to get rich. The profit motive is nothing if not predictable.

Traditionally, corporate climbers are motivated by things such as market forces, economic trends, and a desire to fill holes in their portfolios. In contrast, people who identify personally with their work draw from a different well. Inspired by their convictions, values, and beliefs, they see opportunities that others miss—insights, epiphanies, and germs of ideas as Hatkoff called them—and they stick with them long after extraction-minded peers lose interest or fail. Because contributory leaders see growth and financial prosperity less as goals in and of themselves than as by-products that fuel further opportunities to realize their personal ambitions, extraction has a way of following contribution in a virtuous cycle.

Such is the case with the Tribeca Film Festival. Back in 2001, the world was already saturated with film festivals. Be it Sundance, Cannes, Toronto, Venice, or any of the thousands of other events serving every industry niche and corner of the globe, the world had no need for another film festival. But in the wake of the terrorist attacks of 9/11, with their community in crisis, De Niro, Rosenthal, and Hatkoff were driven to get people back on the street. For the first time, a film festival made sense. According to Hatkoff, Rosenthal summed it up best: "The world didn't need another film festival, but Tribeca did."

Hatkoff elaborates: "From the outset, the festival wasn't about for profit or not for profit. Just like Dinner Downtown, it was for a purpose—one clear purpose: Getting people back to normalcy after a terrorist attack. Festivals aid understanding, build empathy via storytelling, and help cultivate virtues."

By December 2001, the trio had decided to launch the Tribeca Film Festival. There was one outstanding issue: Where to begin? Time being of the essence, they had committed themselves to orchestrating an event in spring 2002, just a few months later. But with no funds, no sponsors, and only one obvious venue (at that time Lower Manhattan had only one theater), the first festival almost didn't happen.

During the next few months, the cofounders of the Tribeca Film Festival worked tirelessly to plan a massive event in the streets of New York City. In a normal year, it would have been hard enough; 2002, in the immediate wake of 9/11, was anything but normal. Phone numbers were disconnected, old contacts had relocated, and vendors had gone out of business. But personal ambition is hard to stop. During those months, logic went out the window, passion went into overdrive, and as the date drew near, almost anything seemed possible—including failure.

"From a financial standpoint, the idea of raising sponsorship funds in 90 days to put on a multimillion-dollar event was ambitious to say the least," says Hatkoff. "We almost failed. We were inside of 24 hours of postponing when new sponsors called."

One was Nancy Smith, then vice president of global media, sponsorship, and events

at American Express. Based just around the corner in Lower Manhattan, American Express was hit hard when the towers collapsed. Eleven employees were killed,[15] and the company's headquarters at Three World Financial Center—immediately adjacent to the World Trade Center—sustained extensive damage.[16] Smith and other American Express employees would be unable to return to their offices until repairs were completed in spring 2002.

Hatkoff recounts: "Nancy called and she said, 'Craig, you don't know me, but I run events for American Express. We hear you are doing a festival. We need to be your partner. We're going to help you build this.'"

American Express was aiming to bring its employees back to its headquarters around the same time as Hatkoff and his cofounders' film festival. Both called Lower Manhattan home, and both shared the same passion: revitalizing the neighborhood.

Finding a corporate partner that also had a personal stake in reviving the neighborhood turned out to be crucial to the festival's success. With American Express's financial backing and the help of some 1,000 volunteers, the inaugural Tribeca Film Festival was an overwhelming success, screening some 140 films—many in local school and college auditoriums—and drawing an estimated 150,000 people to Lower Manhattan.[17] The biggest attraction: a family-themed street fair featuring child-friendly films that for many of those who attended was the first time they had gone out in the neighborhood since 9/11.

———————————

The Tribeca Film Festival has become one of the premier global film festivals. Beyond the in-person attendees, the festival reaches nearly 4 million engaged audience members online.[18] Each year, the event drives revenue back into local businesses, contributing to rather than extracting from the community it was founded to help. Although Hatkoff says the festival will always honor 9/11, the cofounders have adapted and innovated to find new ways to help the festival flourish and keep

Lower Manhattan top of mind among film fans, such as audience-judged awards and a Virtual Arcade, where contestants can submit virtual reality, 360-degree, and augmented reality projects.

"The mission is to help people find meaning and get back on their feet after an unspeakable trauma," says Hatkoff. "As Jane often says, it's also about moving forward and finding new memories in Lower Manhattan."

Of course, there are still plenty of other film festivals, perhaps even more now than there were in 2002. And some of them also have charitable roots. But the Tribeca Film Festival's creation, survival, and rise to prominence in a saturated market is a profound testament to the ongoing ambition of its cofounders, who have defied the odds in their efforts to breathe life back into their neighborhood by contributing their personal talents to a meaningful cause. From the first day they set out, De Niro, Rosenthal, and Hatkoff have never stopped building modern legacies for their film festival, their community, and themselves.

Cofounder Craig Hatkoff, Tribeca Film Festival.

Image above: Splash News/Alamy
Image below: Courtesy of Tribeca Film Festival

In building your modern legacy, what contribution will you make?

By harnessing their ambition to give back to their community, the cofounders of the Tribeca Film Festival show what it means to take work personally. "Doing your best is taking the action because you love it, not because you're expecting a reward," says Don Miguel Ruiz, the author of *The Four Agreements*. "Most people do exactly the opposite. They only take action when they expect a reward, and they don't enjoy the action, and that's the reason they don't do their best." When you enjoy your work so much that it becomes a reward in and of itself, your modern legacy takes shape naturally.

De Niro, Rosenthal, and Hatkoff weren't just looking for a reward when they founded the Tribeca Film Festival. They did their best because they cared about the cause and enjoyed the work. As a result, their enduring efforts over the years illustrate the myriad benefits of building a modern legacy that is based on contribution rather than extraction. Because they take their work personally, they are able to mobilize an audience around a shared set of values, attract A-list partners, and engage audiences in a festival that continues to evolve and thrive.

Take a moment to reflect on your legacy in the making. Beyond extracting, what are you contributing? Are you emotionally invested in your work? If you are not, start by identifying where your ambitions and values intersect. Then ask yourself how you could apply your passion and skill to contribute something the world needs. With your ambitions and values in focus, you'll be ready for the next step: navigating the inevitable challenges that obstruct your path.

The Tribeca Film Festival, like the Tribute in Light display to the right and the Freedom Tower to the left, serve as symbols of New York City's resilience in the aftermath of 9/11.

Susan Candelario/Alamy

(1) **Contribution Before Extraction**
THE TRIBECA FILM FESTIVAL
Established 2002

(2) # Opportunities Out of Obstacles

GIRLS WHO CODE

Established 2012

(3) **Lead, Don't Manage**
NYX COSMETICS
Established 1999

RESHMA SAUJANI ISN'T FAZED by failure; she's inspired by it. The founder of Girls Who Code, a nonprofit on a mission to equip girls with computing skills, and the author of *Women Who Don't Wait in Line*, Saujani found her way into computer programming as a result of personal ambition that initially fell short. In fact, looking further back, it was someone else's failure that first inspired her to take the path she is on today.

"I saw Hillary Clinton give her first concession speech when she ran her first campaign to be president of the United States," Saujani recalls. "She said something very inspiring: 'Just because I failed doesn't mean you shouldn't try too.'"

The year was 2010. Disillusioned with her lucrative job in the financial services industry, Saujani, whose parents emigrated to the United States from Uganda in the 1970s, decided to quit and run for the U.S. House of Representatives.

"Seeing everything this country did for my family inspired me to want to give back someday through public service," she says.

Advised to wait her turn by the political establishment, Saujani, just 34 years old at the time, forged ahead, leading an inspired campaign. She captured an endorsement from the *New York Daily News* and received several mentions in the *New York Times*, and CNBC touted her race as one of the hottest in the country. Despite high hopes, however, Saujani was clobbered in the primary election, earning just 19 percent of the vote.

"I had convinced a lot of people I was going to win," she recalls. "On Election Day, I remember clutching my father's hand, watching the television screen."

Broke, feeling humiliated, and ostracized by those in her own party who had advised her not to run in the first place, Saujani could have given up and returned to her old job and its ample paycheck. Instead, she assessed the highs and lows of her campaign, looking for ways to rechannel her ambition to be of service. Among the highlights: Saujani was a pioneer in leveraging new technologies to get voters to the polls.

Though technology did not win her the primary, Saujani's focus on the field had paid

off in various other ways. As the first to use apps such as Square and NationBuilder in the political sphere, she introduced new ways to raise funds and inspire voters. Despite her underdog status, those innovative efforts garnered national media attention and generated $1.6 million in donations. Most notably, drawing the public's attention to new job opportunities in the tech sector made her aware of a glaring gender imbalance in that industry.

"When you run for office, you end up visiting a lot of schools," she explains. "I was going to lots of robotics labs and computer science classes, and I would often see a bunch of boys all clamoring to be the next Steve Jobs or Mark Zuckerberg. I remember thinking to myself, 'Where are all the girls?' and that question stayed with me."

———————

Many of the stories we hear at The Legacy Lab begin with nagging questions such as the one that stuck with Saujani. Nagging questions are a telltale sign of a nascent

personal ambition. Such thoughts tend to be loaded with personal significance even when they seem unsolvable. In fact, these lingering, seemingly unsolvable questions can be ideal for starting a modern legacy brand.

In business and in life, short-term thinkers tend to take the easy way, dodging obstacles and looking for the path of least resistance. Hooked on instant gratification, they settle for shortcuts. Averse to criticism and failure, they avoid risk. Those with a longer view understand that the reward is generally commensurate with the effort expended. One "personal" way modern legacy builders stay focused on their long-term ambitions is by reframing the obstacles in their paths as opportunities. One might call this "taking the hard way," but there's no better method for creating lasting change than paving your own way while others stay on the beaten path. After all, modern legacy building is as much a way as it is a where.

Saujani, for example, is not a professional software coder, though today tens of thousands of young women have her to thank for introducing them to the field. After losing the primary, Saujani reflected on the paucity

Founder and CEO Reshma Saujani, Girls Who Code.

Image courtesy of Girls Who Code

of women she'd seen in computer programming. Statistically, the long-term picture wasn't good. By 2020, there will be 1.4 million jobs available in computing-related fields. U.S. graduates, however, are on track to fill only 29 percent of those jobs. Worse, unless something changes, only 3 percent of those jobs will go to women.

This, Saujani realized, was her obstacle and her opportunity. Technology presents an incredible career opportunity for the next generation of women if only they understand their own potential and can find a way in. By helping introduce girls to coding—in essence, blazing a path through an obstacle she encountered in her personal path and creating an opportunity for herself and others—Saujani saw a way to give back and drive the kind of societal change she had hoped to make in politics.

Borrowing a friend's conference room for office space, Saujani redirected her campaign skills and passion for public service into launching Girls Who Code. Her modern legacy ambition: to "inspire, educate, and equip girls with the computing skills to pursue twenty-first-century opportunities."

"I spent about all of 2011 and half of 2012 working to understand the problem: Why was there a lack of women in the field of computer science?" she recalls. "My passion for this topic was rooted in creating greater economic opportunity. In the technology sector, where jobs were growing, where a person could make a lot of money as a software engineer, where the related income could help to move a family up to the middle class, why were women so badly underrepresented?"

Saujani began to explore what it would take to put together a curriculum aimed at young women. She focused on identifying women with an interest in technology and inspiring them to pursue coding. The trends weren't in her favor. In 1984, 37 percent of all computer science graduates were women. Today, the number is about 18 percent. In fact, only 26 percent of advanced placement (AP) computer science test takers are women.

Nevertheless, at a time when the majority of college students are women, the majority of those in the labor force are women, and more than 40 percent of breadwinners are women, Saujani saw the lack of women in coding as a huge opportunity.

"It is not an aptitude issue," she points out. "Girls outperform boys in math and science. The problem is that from the time they're very young, girls are actively choosing to not participate in the field."

In 2015, only about 10,000 women in the United States graduated college with a degree in computer science. Only 1 in 10 American schools even offered computer science as a major. Recognizing that girls are 40 percent more likely to major in computer science if they take the AP computer science exam, Saujani began looking for ways to introduce girls to computer programming at a younger age—specifically, between 13 and 17—before the AP exam.

"At Girls Who Code, we are offering an alternative education opportunity through an after-school program and a summer program," she says. "We are stepping in and giving girls experience with and exposure to computer science education starting in high school. We are also working to set a high expectation that they'll major in it in college and then go to work in the industry."

> ## "From one dream can emerge new, better dreams filled with amazing possibility."

Saujani is making headway fast. Over the last five years, Girls Who Code has grown into a national movement, with sponsors and programs in all 50 states.

"Between our summer immersion program, the Girls Who Code Clubs, the book series, and creating platforms for our alumni to connect and communicate with each other, we are building a fully networked and supported organization," she says. "We introduce girls to the topic and impart lifelong knowledge. We give them access to internships. We create a sisterhood of support to help make sure that the girls do not give up. When the girls run into cultural or gender barriers that they will inevitably face and feel deterred from wanting to do this anymore, we have role models who can encourage them along. We are building this one piece at a time, creating strong foundations for a more sustainable solution."

What started with 20 girls in 2012 has grown to more than 50,000. Today, Girls Who Code offers many of its students the opportunity to work at major tech firms in their own regions. An impressive 90 percent of the program's summer alumni intend to major or minor in computer science.

"When I was running for office, I always felt like I was running up a hill; it was very hard to catch a break," says Saujani.

"In contrast, with Girls Who Code, it has so much meaning in it that a lot of people want to help support it by building this with us. It's very rewarding to see and be a part of."

By adapting her personal passions to new circumstances, Saujani stands out as an example of how modern legacy builders create opportunities out of the obstacles they confront in their personal lives. When her political career stalled and she felt there was no path to follow, Saujani blazed her own trail, ultimately creating a way forward for others and herself. At times impeded and inspired by failure, Saujani found her own way—*the hard way*—to build her modern legacy.

"I am probably making more impact, with lasting implications, than if I had been elected," she says. "Being rejected, feeling upset, failing, and seeing dreams not work out should never break you. From one dream can emerge new, better dreams filled with amazing possibility."

FAST FACTS | WOMEN IN TECH

ONLY 26% of AP Computer Science test-takers are women

ABOUT 10,000 women graduated with a degree in computer science

HOWEVER

more than **40%** OF ALL U.S. BREADWINNERS *are women*

Source: Girls Who Code

In building your modern legacy, how can you take the hard way?

When Saujani set out to change computer programming, she knew very little about the industry. Despite that, she identified an obstacle that was important to her and blazed a path through it that others could follow. Can you do the same thing yourself?

First, identify an obstacle you want to solve. Seek out the problems no one has been able to fix and don't let the failure of others prevent your success. The more personal that obstacle is to you, the more willing you will be to invest the hard work necessary to create lasting change rather than take the expedient way out.

If you have trouble identifying an obstacle, let your everyday observations be your field research. Rather than letting a lack of experience stand in your way, how could fresh eyes help you spot obstacles that others take for granted? Begin with your career, community, and hobbies. Any obstacle that draws your attention probably will be personal to you at some level.

Though Saujani set out with a long-term personal ambition to give back through public service, she found herself drawn to a largely overlooked problem she observed on the campaign trail: introducing girls to computer science. Having no experience in the tech industry would have been an easy excuse for ignoring such a tough challenge, but instead, Saujani took the hard way, cracked the code, and turned an obstacle into an opportunity.

Like Saujani, the next modern legacy builder in this chapter was self-assured enough to harness a personal ambition in the name of solving a problem. In this case, though, the problem was even closer to home.

Reshma Saujani, speaking at a Women in Tech event hosted by Girls Who Code. As a result of Saujani's efforts, what began as a small group of 20 girls in 2012 is now a growing movement of more than 50,000.

Richard Levine/Alamy

1 Contribution Before Extraction
THE TRIBECA FILM FESTIVAL
Established 2002

2 Opportunities Out of Obstacles
GIRLS WHO CODE
Established 2012

3 # Lead, Don't Manage

NYX COSMETICS

Established 1999

TONI KO MAY NOT be a household name, but she is a poster child for a new generation of ambitious modern legacy builders. In 2016, Ko's passionate brand-building skills earned her the fifty-seventh spot on *Forbes* magazine's list of the richest self-made women in the United States, landing between Beyoncé (number 56) and Taylor Swift (number 60).[19]

Growing up in the family cosmetics business, Ko understood the industry even as a child from helping out at her parents' store.

"At a very young age, I was learning how to merchandise," she recalls. "How to use color in displays to attract shoppers, apply sensory design to fully engage consumers with products, and integrate functional design to help employees restock merchandise more efficiently."

As she grew up and began using cosmetics herself, her experience as a consumer only deepened her insight. Working for her parents without pay, however, meant she could not afford premium brands. As her peers started earning their own income, she recalls being embarrassed to stand around in groups in front of the mirror to put on makeup.

"My friends would take out their beautiful M•A•C and Lancôme products," she says. "I would take out my drugstore products. I was embarrassed. I didn't want to take out my $4, $5, or $6 hot pink or neon green tubes of mascara. My products screamed drugstore products."

> *"I learned the best way to achieve my ambition and get the job done was to just do it. Less talk. More action."*

From her personal experience, Ko knew that the industry needed a brand of cosmetics that was affordable but did not look or feel like conventional drugstore products. Since no one else was doing it, she decided to do it herself. Her objective was to upgrade the

quality of the packaging of the affordable products without raising the price, allowing girls like her to avoid the same embarrassing moments in front of their peers.

Informed by her bruised ego as a kid, Ko's more mature ego did not hesitate to take the lead in finding a solution.

———————————

Ko's personal ambition to leave the family business and start her own brand took confidence and independence—qualities that can be hard to find in today's short-term business climate. For most of the twentieth century, successful brands have focused on training conventional brand managers: groupthinkers in charge of maintaining the status quo and protecting market share. The results now bog down corporate strategy: decision-making by committee instead of bold leadership, following markets rather than leading them. Somewhere along the line, ego—the self-assuredness to take the lead—became a bad word. But building a modern legacy calls for just that: leaders who

follow their hearts and their heads while everyone else tries to keep up.

"Because of my experience in the business, I knew all that I had to do to lower costs was take all the junk—all the ugliness and all the gaudiness—out of the packaging and make it simple black and white. I knew the problem I was solving. I knew the customer because I was the customer. And I learned the best way to achieve my ambition and get the job done was to just do it. Less talk. More action."

With a little financial help and some warehouse space borrowed from her family, she launched her own independent company: NYX Cosmetics. NYX grew out of Ko's passion to break free from the family business and unleash her own ideas in an industry she already knew inside out. As a statement of her strength, independence, and empowerment, she named the brand NYX after a Greek goddess she describes as emblematic of her desire "to combine courage and beauty."

"I have always been very hands-on with my work," she says. "In the beginning, at

NYX, I used to test all the products on myself. When going to nearby trade shows, in Las Vegas, for example, I would haul the merchandise in my car, load it, and unload it myself and assemble my own booth too. From the outset, at NYX I was the pricing, products, and promotions group. I was the everything group."

When pitching NYX at industry conventions failed to capture the attention of national distributors, Ko changed course, networking until she reached decision makers who could offer her product broader distribution.

"On my own, I had grown NYX to the point where it was sold in nearly 4,000 of the available 5,000 small beauty supply accounts such as ABC Beauty Supply, King's Beauty Supply, Lee's Beauty Supply, and others," Ko recalls. "I was doing about $25 million to $30 million in revenue. To grow further, I would have to get into national chain accounts: CVS Pharmacy, Walgreens, Target, maybe ULTA and Sephora someday too."

The solution: Ko began courting investment partners who had relationships with national retailers, ultimately finding an investor and launching NYX at several nationwide chains. Even as NYX was taking off across the country, Ko's hands-on method of leadership allowed her to keep her finger on the pulse of her brand, and she encouraged her customers to share their ideas.

Here is an example: "There was one item we were going to discontinue—a white-colored jumbo eye shadow pencil that had a slight texture to it," she says. "Seemingly out of nowhere, this product started to sell at a very high quantity. In the beginning, we weren't sure why. Shortly thereafter, we saw that YouTubers were using our product as an eye shadow base."

Ko then sent her products to fans with their own YouTube channels (a novel approach at the time).

"We would send out one lipstick, and they were so happy that they would, in turn, support us by making 10 videos," Ko recalls. "If one video was seen by 10,000 people and you multiplied that by 10 videos, we would quickly get to 100,000 views. Now, multiply that by 10 of our fans and bloggers all doing the same thing, and not just for one product

Founder Toni Ko, NYX Cosmetics, PERVERSE Sunglasses, and Butter Ventures.

Image courtesy of Toni Ko

but for lots of them. The impressions that came at effectively no cost were priceless."

———————————

By taking on leadership roles in every aspect of her growing business—from testing her own products and pitching them at trade shows to contacting customers and courting major investors—Ko was able to grow NYX from a borrowed space in her family's warehouse to a national powerhouse. Her bootstrap success ultimately forced established brands to rethink the ways they approached affordable makeup. After selling NYX Cosmetics for an estimated $500 million to L'Oréal, the largest beauty conglomerate in the world, Ko moved on to her next challenge: PERVERSE sunglasses, a line of high-fashion $30 to $75 eyewear intended to disrupt a category long dominated by overpriced fashion labels.[20]

"After I sold NYX, I planned to retire from work life," she recalls. "I thought I would sit on a beach, drink margaritas, and do nothing. But when I did that, I got bored. Fast. I am happiest when working on building something I love."

Ko also launched a small investment firm called Butter Ventures intended to support the passions of other young founders, entrepreneurs, and future leaders with investments of about $30,000. Notably, she focuses her investment strategy on inspired, ambitious women much like herself.

In each of Ko's various pursuits she exhibits the traits of a leader, not a manager. When launching NYX, she set out to solve a problem she had experienced personally: providing an affordable alternative to cheap, garish cosmetics. She was the one setting up booths at trade shows and finding her way into the boardrooms of national retailers. Then, rather than resting on her laurels after selling her first company, she went right back out and started a new one. At Butter Ventures, she handpicks young female entrepreneurs like herself to invest in.

Every decision along the way bears Ko's personal touch, the fingerprints of a leader driven by personal ambition and ego rather than by committee. In the process, she is creating a modern legacy built on solving problems herself, a legacy in the making she continues to author each day.

In building your modern legacy, how will you free your ego?

The word *ego* sometimes gets a bad rap because it is associated with overconfidence or being full of oneself. But in today's short-term business environment, where big brands are often slow and risk-averse, ego can be nimble and courageous. In a world that seeks to slow you down, ego can move you forward. Moreover, your ego is uniquely personal—it is what makes you *you*—and no competitor can copy that.

Ko, for example, is able to lead with ego because all of her long-term ambitions tie back to something in her personal life, whether it is NYX Cosmetics, PERVERSE sunglasses, or Butter Ventures. In each case, she takes her work personally and believes in herself rather than blindly following someone else's ambitions.

How can you set your ego free? Start by examining whether the choices you're making feel brave. Are you doing only what's popular or are you doing what you know is right? Are you managing toward compromise or leading from your gut and intuition? Rather than managing someone else's goals, let your instincts and ambitions lead the way.

Toni Ko knew the cosmetics industry needed a brand that was affordable but did not look or feel like a conventional drugstore brand. No one else was doing it, so she decided to do it herself.

Image courtesy of Toni Ko

 **Summation**

At any given time, each of us has an array of personal ambitions. Maybe you desire to improve a community, revolutionize an industry, or change the direction of society at large. Maybe all of the above, all at once. To paraphrase Walt Whitman, "We are large, we contain multitudes." Fortunately, rather than overwhelming us as assigned tasks tend to do, long-term personal ambitions have a way of motivating us. Because our ambitions are inherently *personal*, they're aligned with our personal beliefs and desires. Taking work personally is literally in our nature. This is why personal ambitions inspire us to work harder, persist longer, and reach farther: They mean more to us.

Why is something so natural so hard for so many? The reason is as simple as it is disheartening: Short-term goals seduce us with offers of immediate gratification, whereas long-term ambitions appear to pay off only over time. Sound familiar? It's part of the short-term thinker's blind spot we discussed in the Introduction to this book.

Modern legacy builders understand that working toward long-term ambition does not only afford strategic benefits such as greater effort and dedication; when you love what you do, the labor is a continuous reward in and of itself. We encourage you to use the stories and lessons in this chapter as an inspiration for identifying your own personal ambition and building your modern legacy.

Consider the transformative power of a long-term personal ambition.

The Tribeca Film Festival is not just another film festival for Robert De Niro, Jane Rosenthal, and Craig Hatkoff. Instead, it's an evolving labor of love borne out of the ambition to give back to their neighborhood. This personal connection is why the event continues to evolve and find new ways to engage and inspire its community year after year.

Reshma Saujani, rather than becoming another financial services executive or politician, is conquering an obstacle she observed on the campaign trail. Girls Who Code has introduced tens of thousands of young women to a segment of the tech industry that already is benefiting from her success.

Although Toni Ko could have climbed the ranks and managed a conventional cosmetics brand, she chose to lead from her own experience, be a lifelong contributor with brands such as NYX Cosmetics and PERVERSE sunglasses, and invest in other young female entrepreneurs like herself through Butter Ventures.

In the face of diverse challenges, each of these modern legacy builders is driven by a long-term personal ambition to make a unique and durable difference. If they had not taken their work personally— if they had left their jobs at the office and not sought to make a significant contribution—our world would not be the same.

THE LEGACY BUILDER'S
BALANCE SHEET

Gauge Your Ikigai

Ikigai, a Japanese concept meaning "reason for being," is a personal measurement tool that was introduced to us by Brent Bushnell, cofounder of Two Bit Circus. A high-tech, interactive gaming and entertainment brand, Two Bit Circus is also dedicated to inspiring the next generation of young inventors by adding art to science, technology, engineering, and math (making STEAM from STEM).

"*Ikigai* is a Japanese concept that I just love," says Bushnell. "It's a concept around happiness. It suggests that you will find happiness when you can:

a.   do what you love,
b.   do what you are good at,
c.   do what you can be paid for, and
d.   do what the world needs."

"*Ikigai* lives at the intersection of all of those things," he says. "It is unfair to tell a kid to only do what they love. Why? Because we also live in a world that revolves around money. So traditionally in Western society, you could choose to make a buck or make a difference. Or, more holistically, according to *ikigai*, you can do both while also doing what you love and what you are good at. To find *ikigai* requires having all four aspects."

So what exactly is Two Bit Circus? Search the Web and you're likely to find all sorts of explanations for what the brand does, from "engineering entertainment" to a "make tank" focused on products at the crossroads of amusement and education. You'll see creative work for the film *La La Land*, the

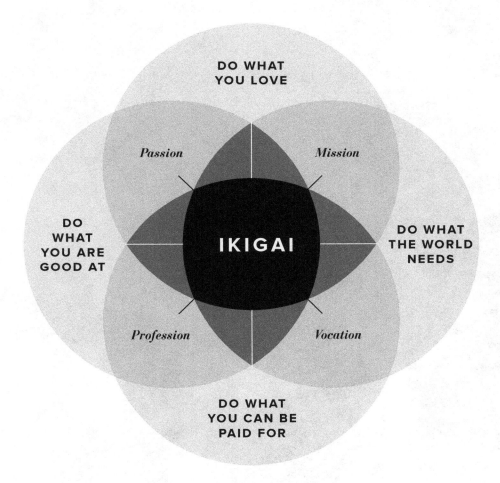

Get Centered

Drawn from Japanese philosophy, *ikigai* is an elegant visualization tool composed of four complementary aspirations that all overlap to reveal your "reason for being." Brent Bushnell arrived at his personal *ikigai*, Two Bit Circus, after reflecting on his aspirations. To discover your own *ikigai*, ask yourself what you love to do, what you are good at, what you can be paid for, and what the world needs, then examine where your responses overlap and complement each other.

Inspired by work from Emmy van Deurzen and others

Cofounders of Two Bit Circus, Brent Bushnell (right) and Eric Gradman, combining high tech with high fun to bring STEAM to life.

Image courtesy of Two Bit Circus

Rio Olympics, and the NFL. Or click on the music video "This Too Shall Pass" and be spellbound by the four-minute-long Rube Goldberg contraption many from their team built for the band OK Go. Or simply imagine a group of mad scientists who ran away with the circus. Two Bit Circus provides its cofounders with their own unique reason for being right in the *ikigai* sweet spot.

Take the time to gauge your own *ikigai.* Assess your strengths in each dimension: what you love, what you're good at, what you can be paid for, and what the world needs. Does your current pursuit place you at the heart of all four aspirations? If it does not, what could you do to calibrate the aspirations that are out of balance? Or are you so far off the mark that it might take a career change to reorient yourself into the center? Identifying new ways to bring more of yourself to the way you lead will make your life and your work more personal, meaningful, and rewarding.

CHAPTER TWO

Behave Your Beliefs

"There is a job and then there is a calling. We want to hire people who aren't just looking for jobs, they're looking for a calling."

| BRIAN CHESKY |

Cofounder, Chief Executive Officer, and Head of Community, Airbnb[1]

THERE'S A STORY Brian Chesky tells about meeting with Peter Thiel, the well-known Silicon Valley venture capitalist. It was 2012, Airbnb's fourth year in business, and Thiel had just granted $150 million in Series C financing to the ambitious peer-to-peer house-sharing brand created by Chesky and fellow cofounders Joe Gebbia and Nathan Blecharczyk.[2] During Thiel's visit to the brand's San Francisco office, Chesky asked the venture capitalist for his single-most important piece of advice.

"Don't fuck up the culture," said Thiel.

The investor explained that Airbnb's strong culture was one of the main reasons he was backing the brand and that all companies inevitably screw up their cultures when they get too big. Somewhere between scrappy upstart and industry leader, the brand culture often fails and the company loses its way.

Thiel couldn't have found a better audience. Already known for his devotion to Airbnb's internal culture (the CEO personally interviewed Airbnb's first 300 employees),[3] Chesky sent out a company-wide e-mail elaborating on the topic. In the e-mail, which soon went viral, Chesky stressed the importance of building culture by "upholding our core values in everything we do":

There are days when it's easy to feel the pressure of our own growth expectations. Other days when we need to ship product. Others still where we are dealing with the latest government relations issue. It's easy to get consumed by these. And they are all very important. But compared to culture, they are relatively short term. These problems will come and go. But culture is forever.[4]

Next, Chesky articulated a rallying cry built on a deeply held brand belief: "Belong anywhere."[5] Guided in part by beliefs like these, Airbnb's culture has thrived in the face of significant challenges. Though the brand initially ignored naysayers who objected to its rental model, Chesky now encourages his employees to engage community members and government regulators to develop cooperative solutions.[6] After incidents of racial bias among consumers, in 2016 Airbnb hired former Attorney General Eric Holder[7] and began working with Harvard University professor Robert Livingston,[8] an antibias expert, to help address all forms of discrimination across the brand. In the interest of transparency, Chesky has regularly posted candid blogs describing improvements, pledging to do better, and even apologizing for shortcomings.[9]

Today, with more than 2,500 employees,[10] a market value of $30 billion, and nearly $3 billion in annual revenue,[11] Airbnb is getting its business right. For proof that the brand is still getting its culture right, look no further than its human resource department: For every job opening, Airbnb reports receiving some 200 applicants.[12]

Rather than just singing his brand's praises and putting out fires the way many figurehead leaders do, Chesky devotes himself to reinforcing his brand's values internally and encouraging colleagues to express those values through their unique behaviors. His dedication is telling of the second transformation in the modern legacy mindset: from attitudinal posturing to behaving your beliefs.

Transformation:

Nearsighted brand leaders imagine their brands first from the outside in, believing that attitude—what they say and how they posture—matters most.

Leaders with the modern legacy mindset build from the inside out in accordance with beliefs that drive behaviors because actions matter more than words alone.

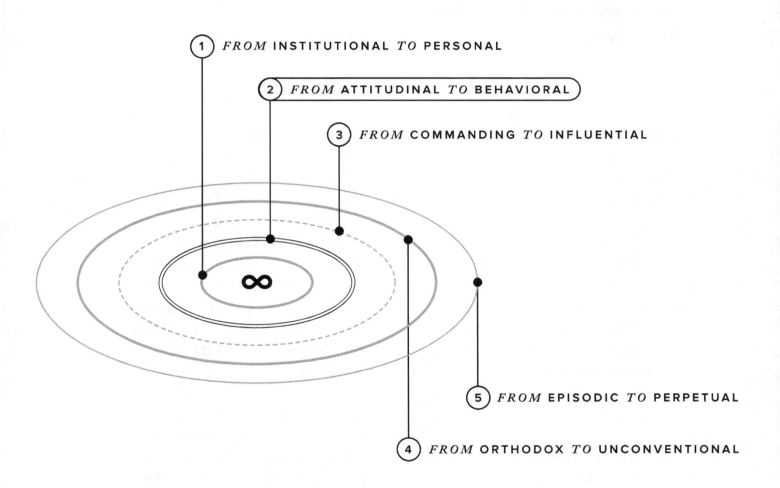

1. FROM INSTITUTIONAL *TO* PERSONAL

2. FROM ATTITUDINAL *TO* BEHAVIORAL

3. FROM COMMANDING *TO* INFLUENTIAL

5. FROM EPISODIC *TO* PERPETUAL

4. FROM ORTHODOX *TO* UNCONVENTIONAL

Once you've identified a long-term personal ambition, who will share in it with you?

Chapter 1 of the book emphasized the importance of leaders following their own personal ambition. Chapter 2 now examines how leaders at The Honest Company, The Bluebird Cafe, and The Ritz-Carlton Hotel Company share their passion and enlist colleagues to help craft their modern legacies. It's one thing to have a dream or know your long-term personal ambitions, but few people realize their dreams on their own. To migrate from dreaming to doing, they need the help of others who believe and behave the way they do. Harnessing beliefs and behavior to build your modern legacy starts from the inside out—with a strong brand culture.

A brand's culture is a vehicle for its values, though it won't drive itself. Nevertheless, too many brands treat their culture as if it were on autopilot. Although they start out with a virtuous pledge or a set of values,

this rarely amounts to more than lip service. The reality is that most businesses relegate "culture" to boilerplate language in human resources handbooks. Even if employees can recite those handbooks word for word, that isn't culture; it's an echo chamber.

This is the problem with the way conventional brand leaders generally treat their culture: They devote more time to attitude than to action. This posturing creates a disconnect between beliefs and behaviors, and we're all familiar with the consequences when companies don't live by their words. At best, employees can regurgitate a meaningless mishmash of slogans, jargon, and corporate-speak. At worst, a negative culture emerges on its own and things get toxic. And when a brand culture goes bad, it takes everyone down with it.

Modern legacy builders understand that a strong culture is built on behaving your beliefs. Culture is the social bonding agent between intentions and deeds, the glue that makes the whole greater than the sum of its parts. When you get your culture right, it scales quickly as you grow, enabling better short-term decision-making. Though culture is famously difficult to create and maintain, those very qualities are what make it virtually impossible to copy. This explains why culture, done right, is the ultimate competitive advantage.

Because brand culture is critical to the decisions you and your employees will make about products, services, and strategies today, tomorrow, and years into the future, it's important to start building it right from the start. Begin with a core set of beliefs that support your long-term personal ambition. Make them clear and inspiring. In the words of Dee Hock, the founder of Visa, "Simple, clear purpose and principles give rise to complex, intelligent behavior. Complex rules and regulations give rise to simple, stupid behavior."[13]

Next, because words go only so far, leverage brand beliefs to inspire employee behaviors. In search of new ways to bring brand cultures to life, in this chapter we look to Christopher Gavigan, cofounder (along with Jessica Alba, Brian Lee, and Sean Kane) of The Honest Company, a modern legacy brand on a quest to create a cleaner world; Amy Kurland, champion of singer-songwriters and founder of The Bluebird Cafe (as well as her handpicked successor, Erika Wollam Nichols); and founding member and chairman emeritus of The Ritz-Carlton Hotel Company, Hervé Humler, who empowers legendary customer service at the iconic luxury hospitality brand. Their stories offer unique insights into how you too can cultivate an enduring brand culture in a short-term world.

By aligning behaviors with brand beliefs, modern legacy builders are finding new ways to migrate from dreaming to doing. When your long-term personal ambition inspires a shared set of brand beliefs that manifests in countless unique employee behaviors, your legacy in the making will thrive.

① Your Culture Is Your Product

THE HONEST COMPANY

Established 2012

② Deeds, Not Words

THE BLUEBIRD CAFE

Established 1982

③ Empower Your Believers

THE RITZ-CARLTON HOTEL COMPANY

Established 1983

THE GUEST LIST at the 2008 launch party for Christopher Gavigan's book *Healthy Child Healthy World* read like a Who's Who of Hollywood, politics, and the music industry. Hosted by *People* magazine, A-list invitees included Tom Hanks, Gwyneth Paltrow, Sheryl Crow, and First Lady Michelle Obama. Gavigan himself, a consumer advocate, would have been starstruck if much of the star power had not already personally contributed essays for his book, a how-to treatise for parents on creating a "cleaner, greener, safer home."

As friends hoisted congratulatory toasts and a photographer from *InStyle* magazine worked the room, actress Jessica Alba weaved her way through the crowd and introduced herself to Gavigan. Eight months pregnant with her first child and recovering from an allergic reaction to laundry detergent, she had an urgent plea.

"Please," she said, explaining that her due date was just a month away. "What do I buy?"

The question was familiar, and Gavigan didn't miss a beat, offering guidance on nontoxic alternatives to mainstream baby products. The two quickly bonded over their shared concerns. Couldn't someone do better? Did all corporations have to behave the same way?

"Parents don't want to be weekend toxicologists," Gavigan says, referring to the daunting task parents face when shopping for consumer packaged goods (CPGs), an industry often maligned for using opaque packaging and harsh chemicals. "They want someone to outsource their trust to."

Gavigan was just that someone. The CEO of a nonprofit promoting nontoxic products and the proud author of a new book on the subject, Gavigan had years of experience in the field. Huddled together that evening in a star-studded hip Hollywood restaurant, neither the first-time author nor the expectant new mother had any idea that their casual encounter would someday lead to what many in the media now describe as a "billion-dollar brand." Looking back, however, the story of how a good idea grew into an industry icon began right then with the connection of two like-minded believers envisioning a better kind of company—a

company that behaved honestly. That night, the culture of a new brand was born.

In the months that followed, Alba continued to consult Gavigan about nontoxic products for her new baby girl. As their friendship grew, the conversation turned from product recommendations to a grander shared ambition: bringing healthier ingredients and honest labeling to the consumer packaged-goods industry.

Devoted to making a difference through legislation, Alba and Gavigan traveled to Washington, D.C., in 2011, lobbying on Capitol Hill for better regulations governing CPGs. Between Alba's celebrity status and Gavigan's stature as a consumer advocate, they figured they had a good chance of getting Congress's attention. Lawmakers, however, didn't listen and once again allowed the American Chemical Society to write its own rules. Disappointed but unfazed, the two friends returned home to California determined to rechannel their efforts into launching their own honest CPG company.

"I felt, here's the moment when a company can actually set the standard," says Gavigan. "We can self-regulate and self-impose the criteria that we believe should be in the marketplace."

"In our mission statement, we don't talk about products. We talk about creating a healthier, safer, happier lifestyle."

Joining forces with cofounders Brian Lee and Sean Kane, Alba and Gavigan launched The Honest Company in 2012. Like the aspirational name they chose, Honest's cofounders wanted their brand to stand out

The Principles of Leading an Honest Company:

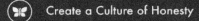

Create a Culture of Honesty

We are serious about honesty—both as it applies to the integrity of our relationships and in being true to you. And, it's a standard we encourage throughout our staff, stakeholders, and customers. But, that's just the beginning. In all we do, we want to make each day a little more fulfilling, inspired, and downright better.

Make Beauty

Your home sets the stage for your life. We design our products that add to the beauty of your surroundings (instead of things you want to hide in drawers and under sinks). We like to play with rich colors, whimsical details, modern shapes, and multi-cultural inspirations.

Outperform

Modern families are busy and everything matters. That's why we craft products that will perform to the highest standards of effectiveness. Products that take care. Products that exceed expectations. Products guaranteed to not only satisfy, but also delight. We are relentless in the pursuit to be attentive to every detail.

Service Matters

We know exceptional service is important, and we intend to go above and beyond, and way over the top. We believe that a deeper level of trust can be built with incredible service. And knowing when to say "sorry," dedicated to making it right . . . all with a super big smile. Serving you better is also about listening and being open to dialogue—that's when we have the opportunity to learn the most (so thank you).

Sustain Life

We believe if you can make an amazing product without harming people or the planet, you should (and we do believe we can). We feel tremendous responsibility to this planet we call home. We are serious about being honest stewards of the natural environment and protectors of the (little) people. Therefore, we seek to inspire new solutions, reduce our collective impact, cause no unnecessary harm, and make products that are as non-toxic and healthy as possible.

Be Accessible

We strive to make our products as affordable as possible. And what's more convenient than having it shipped right to your door? We want every family to have the opportunity to be a part of The Honest Company experience. Accessibility is a promise to openly listen to you & collaborate—so that with you, we can continually become better and always improve.

Pay it Forward

As parents, we teach our kids to be kind and respectful citizens and as a company, we feel it's just as important. We are committed to both individual and corporate social responsibility—taking selfless actions that benefit others. This includes charitable partnerships, working with advocates on promoting policy changes that better protect our children and planet, and supporting the efforts of our employees with paid community service days and direct matches of non-profit donations.

Fun!

We constantly seek ways to create it, have it, and share it as much as possible LOL!

Together we can make it better℠.

Source: The Honest Company

in the CPG industry, imagining it as open and transparent, "a social enterprise with purpose-based DNA." In other words, they wanted Honest's principles to overshadow its products. In fact, contrary to many brands that launch with one iconic product or service and gradually branch out, Honest launched with an entire product line on day 1, introducing 17 nontoxic personal care products in all.

"In our mission statement, we don't talk about products," Gavigan says. "We talk about creating a healthier, safer, happier lifestyle. Our products are the tools we use to educate, empower, and change behavior."

Honest's focus on principles before products exemplifies how modern legacy brands build a strong culture from the inside out by channeling employees' shared beliefs into authentic brand behaviors. The message has resonated with consumers. Today, Honest sells more than 200 nontoxic products, generating some $300 million in revenue.

As Honest takes up more space on retail shelves, however, longstanding CPG titans such as Johnson & Johnson and Unilever are taking stock.[14] As recently as 2016, rumors swirled that Unilever would buy the upstart brand for upward of $1 billion. Expressing gratitude for Honest's good fortune so far but no less ambitious to continue driving change, Gavigan points to the brand's principles as integral to its success.

"Those principles are the foundation of this company," Gavigan says. "That's the promise we are offering the world."

As the task of keeping that promise each and every day falls to its employees, Honest treats its brand culture as its primary product, investing in efforts to ensure that employee behaviors stay true to its core principles. The principles on the previous page have guided The Honest Company through exponential growth since its earliest days, allowing the brand to build its modern legacy from the inside out.

———————————

Big corporations traditionally are known for one iconic product or service, not for their brand values. If you worked at Ford, for example, you built cars. Levi Strauss & Co.? You made jeans. Employees at Ma Bell kept the phone lines up and running. A brand's corporate culture—the internal beliefs and behaviors cultivated behind the scenes—has almost always taken a backseat to the products and services that brand produced. This generally meant that what you made or what you did while at work was what everyone noticed—not the underlying reason you felt a calling to work in the first place.

Culture-driven companies such as The Honest Company are demonstrating that what a brand believes can eclipse what it makes. These modern legacy brands put long-term ambitions before short-term motives, ultimately achieving the kind of success that doesn't always fit within the margins of a quarterly revenue report. In Honest's case, the brand's success has led to heightened consumer awareness and indirectly to industrywide improvements in the way ingredients are selected, sourced, and labeled. Though brands like Honest aren't yet the norm, those which are behaving the best are proving that culture and brand can be synonymous. So long as a brand and its principles remain indistinguishable, culture has a better chance of scaling as the brand grows.

Cofounders Jessica Alba and Christopher Gavigan, The Honest Company. Says Gavigan: "[Our] principles are the foundation of this company."

Image courtesy of The Honest Company

With Honest's rapid growth has come the need to hire—quickly. How has Honest kept brand behaviors in harmony with its principles? By establishing bedrock principles at the outset, standing by them over the years, and diligently hiring employees who share them.

The task of keeping principles and behaviors aligned falls to Gavigan, now Honest's chief purpose officer and the person in charge of company culture. Scaling—making sure that the next 3,500 employees understand and follow the brand's mission as well as the first 350 have—is his biggest concern. To keep everyone pointed in the right direction, Gavigan starts by ensuring that colleagues understand the brand's principles. (Gavigan's book—now a bestseller and one of the brand's unofficial charter documents—is required reading for every new employee.) Finding ways to reinforce the brand's principles through day-to-day decisions is the next step. The goal, says Gavigan, is to make sure everyone

is "grounded in who we are and where we are going," affording the brand a position of clarity and strength.

"We are not going to compromise," he says. Of course, it takes more than sage words on a page to keep grounded as you grow. To maintain a focus on brand principles and behaviors, Gavigan works directly with employees, whether it is in one-on-one training sessions, leadership meetings, or brandwide innovation gatherings, the latter of which are affectionately called "Kombuchas with Christopher."

"I intentionally walk through the office every day and think, 'How do I impact a person to get them more excited about what they're doing at work that's in tune with our mission?'" he says. "Because if I'm not doing that, then they're not getting it."

The benefits of this kind of collective buy-in and shared vision are particularly evident when brands must make tough decisions, such as how to handle nuanced ethical or philosophical issues. As a leader in safe, healthy products, for example, Honest could justly criticize competitors for using caustic ingredients or misleading packaging. Instead, the brand tries to rally consumers and competitors alike toward cleaner, greener ways of doing business. As Gavigan puts it, "Honest would rather shine a light than cast a shadow."

"It would be easy for us to call out other companies for wrongdoings—for being disingenuous, greenwashing, making false statements, or being dishonest in their marketing practices," Gavigan admits. "But I don't think that's the way you build great reputations and become iconic over time. I think it's really our job to lure people by building a bonfire that's purposeful and strong—a bonfire that draws people in through our education, our voice, our tone, our beauty, our design, and our standards."

The glow of Honest's bonfire has drawn a crowd. Although corporate America generally discounts company culture as a "soft" business discipline, Honest provides undeniable evidence of the profound competitive advantages of being disciplined about your beliefs, not just your bottom line. Beyond keeping talent, Honest's ability to rally more and more employees around its core princi-

ples as it grows demonstrates the scalability of a shared set of beliefs. Even as the brand expands in size, reach, and revenue, Honest's founding principles have remained cultural touchstones, guiding brand behavior. Meanwhile, as difficult as culture is to create and maintain, particularly during a company's growth, every brand culture is inherently unique, rendering it impossible for competitors to replicate it. Gavigan says the most inspiring competitive advantage may be that Honest's cultural discipline affords the brand limitless opportunities to express its principles.

"Right now, we are using the products as tools to ignite the conversation," Gavigan explains. "Five years from now, we could be doing something totally different."

In a fiercely competitive CPG landscape in which rivals are quick to emulate products and marketing tactics, Honest will have to continue holding its cultural torch to maintain its position in the industry. First and foremost, this means staying true to its word: keeping Honest honest. To do that, Gavigan and his colleagues are protecting Honest's culture as if it were the brand's bestselling product. Which, in many ways, it is.

In building your modern legacy, how can you let culture be your guide?

Embracing culture as your brand from day 1 means ensuring that your beliefs and behaviors always come first. In The Honest Company's case, those beliefs came before any products were designed. The earlier you get started, the better. Although growing culture from the inside out is a challenge, it's far more difficult to bolt it on after your brand has taken on a life of its own. Fortunately, the myriad competitive advantages of a strong culture mean that a sustained investment will pay for itself many times over as the brand grows and the culture scales with it. Best of all, although products and services can be imitated, your culture cannot be duplicated.

To build brand culture the way Honest has, ask these questions: Beyond products or services, do you know what you're really selling (and why you are selling it)? If you knew culture was your most important product, how much more would you spend on it? Finally, what kinds of tangible investments are you making in your brand's internal culture each day? The true test comes when times are lean. When they face economic hardship, most companies tend to cut from culture first. Modern legacy builders cut from culture last. Even, as in the next example, when it means passing up something of short-term value to ensure the survival of long-term values.

From right, cofounders Christopher Gavigan, Sean Kane, and Brian Lee, bringing culture to life at an all-hands company meeting.

Image courtesy of The Honest Company

---

1 **Your Culture Is Your Product**
THE HONEST COMPANY
Established 2012

2 Deeds, Not Words

THE BLUEBIRD CAFE

Established 1982

3 **Empower Your Believers**
THE RITZ-CARLTON HOTEL COMPANY
Established 1983

BY THE TIME Garth Brooks appeared for his audition at The Bluebird Cafe in 1987, the singer-songwriter had been turned down by some of country music's biggest record labels. Rolling up to The Bluebird's unassuming storefront in suburban Nashville, Brooks walked in, sat down, and began to play.

"I didn't know who he was, but I gave him the highest score I have ever given anybody for the audition," recalls Amy Kurland, The Bluebird's founder and the patron saint of Nashville's singer-songwriter community. Since opening the cafe in 1982, Kurland has always put the music first, ensuring that The Bluebird's doors were open to newcomers. Though Kurland could have booked bigger acts, she believed in Brooks from the start.

"I thought he was lovely and had tremendous presentation," she says of Brooks, then just 26 years old. "He just had that charisma."

When Brooks returned to play before The Bluebird's small, live audience (the cafe's 20 tables, small bar, and eight church pews seat about 100), he got a standing ovation. When he returned again the next year, he got his first record deal.

"Capitol Records, the record label that had already turned him down, was there in person," Kurland recalls. "I mean, they grabbed him, took him down the back hall, and made him agree to sign a record deal with them right there!"

Brooks is not the only country music legend to get a start on The Bluebird's intimate stage. Since the cafe opened in 1982, Vince Gill, Kathy Mattea, Dierks Bentley, Keith Urban, Taylor Swift, and Lady Antebellum have all walked through The Bluebird's doors with the same dream. In each case, the cafe's supportive founder (and manager, booking agent, bartender, janitor, accountant . . .) made sure her doors were open to new acts even if they didn't always fill the seats.

Today, The Bluebird Cafe is one of the world's premier country music venues. It is the kind of place where emerging musicians and stadium-filling stars alike have a chance to perform within arm's reach of their audience. Kurland purposely limited seats in its iconic In the Round circular performance space to protect what she describes as the "incredible, intimate moment of audience and musicians all

est. **1982**

Nashville, Tennessee

twenty TABLES
one SMALL BAR
eight CHURCH PEWS

CAPACITY
100

Vince Gill
Kathy Mattea
Dierks Bentley
Keith Urban
Taylor Swift
Lady Antebellum
& more...

★ ★ ★ ★ ★

...have all
walked
through
The Bluebird
Cafe's doors

The Bluebird Cafe's motto is

Shhh!

It's a listening room.

Source: The Bluebird Cafe

sharing in a way that is less performance than it is community."

"We are a listening room," she stresses. "The Bluebird is much less interested in selling the maximum number of drinks than it is in making sure the musicians are listened to. It is probably the most important thing The Bluebird does."

———————————

To better understand Kurland's unwavering commitment to providing up-and-coming singer-songwriters a space to perform, we have to go back to the beginning—to 1982. Kurland was just out of college when she opened The Bluebird with some money from her grandmother. Though she had worked in restaurants, she confesses she had no idea what she was doing during the first few years. Eager to learn more about running a business, she signed up for extra-curricular courses at the local community college, attending class after working in the kitchen and vacuuming floors at The Bluebird all day.

"The one that impacted me the most was a marketing class where I learned you have to be *one thing*," she says. "You can't be everything to everybody. You have to think about what you do best."

Kurland and The Bluebird are now known for creating a world-famous performance venue for up-and-coming singer-songwriters, but back when she was just getting started, the cafe was just that: a cafe. It didn't even have a place to perform. When a boyfriend suggested that she add a stage so that his band could play, she decided to give it a shot. Little did she know it at the time, but that was when her legacy in the making really began to take shape.

As Bluebird performances began to draw more listeners, Kurland decided to lean into the music. First, she dropped lunch service and added second shows in the evenings—one for up-and-coming songwriters and another for established artists. Audiences kept lining up. Before long, they were cramming to get in. Kurland had found her "one thing": creating a space where musicians could be appreciated by audiences that really listened.

Always one to back up her beliefs with action, Kurland was receptive to ideas that would improve the unique atmosphere and experience of her "listening room." Perhaps the most notable example of this came during a night of drinking when a group of singer-songwriters (several of whom are now in the Country Music Hall of Fame) asked if they could perform in the center of the cafe, eye to eye with the audience, instead of up on the stage against the wall. Not only would the performance be more intimate, the music would be the center of attention. Although nobody but Kurland remembered making the suggestion the next day, she followed through. The now-legendary In the Round performance space was born.

Guardian angel of The Bluebird's "listening room," Kurland resisted adding seats even as crowds swelled outside her doors. With just 100 audience members, performances took on a reverent dimension uncommon to most live music spaces. "Shhh!" became the cafe's motto. It wasn't just talk. Under Kurland's watchful eye, noisy audience members were kept in line.

> ## "I knew I wanted this place to exist long after I was gone."

Year after year, decade after decade, Kurland watched over The Bluebird's one-of-a-kind listening room, content to let other aspects of the business follow the one thing The Bluebird does best.

"The music is the thing that makes The Bluebird perfect," she says. "The Bluebird is small. Musicians can't make the most money here. We don't have a greenroom, and we don't have a fruit basket for them, but we give musicians and songwriters the things they want most in the world: to be listened to and the chance for their performance to perhaps carry them to the next level."

As Kurland neared retirement, however, the brand she built and the reverent space she had cultivated faced an existential crisis. If Kurland sold The Bluebird to the highest bidder, she knew its unique place in the culture of country music would not survive under a traditional restaurateur or bar owner.

Talking about brand beliefs is one thing, but providing them with the constant care and feeding necessary to keep them alive and well is where most companies fall short. This is particularly the case when money is on the line. Looking to sell her beloved cafe and retire, Kurland knew the decision she was about to make would be one of the most significant of her life.

———————

Thinking back, Kurland recalls the questions running through her mind as she approached retirement. "When I decided after 25 years I was tired of the harder parts of running a venue—fixing the ice machine and taking care of the plumbing, which was my job too—I started to think, 'How could this go on after me?' I couldn't sell it to an individual or even a big business because there is far more money in running a sports bar than running a listening room."

At that point, Kurland made a selfless decision. Determined to keep The Bluebird as it was rather than see it transformed into a sports bar or, worse, a sad parody of itself under an unscrupulous new owner, she decided she would be willing to relinquish any profits from selling the cafe if she could find a way to pass The Bluebird forward to an owner who appreciated it as much as she did. Reaching out to the Nashville Songwriters Association International (NSAI)—the world's largest not-for-profit trade songwriters association—she spoke to Erika Wollam Nichols, a former Bluebird employee and the NSAI's director of development.[15] Having weighed the decision carefully, Kurland proposed donating The Bluebird to the NSAI.

Honored by the offer, Wollam Nichols and the NSAI, which is "committed to protecting the rights and future of the profession of songwriting," insisted on paying Kurland a fair price. Like the faithful hero of so many of those country songs she had listened to

In the Round over the years, Kurland got a happy ending.

Back at The Bluebird, the band played on. By entrusting her business to a like-minded owner capable of carrying her modern legacy forward, Kurland's last act as The Bluebird's owner ensured that the cafe would survive, maintaining its core fan base and authentic place in the culture of country music.

"I knew I wanted this place to exist long after I was gone," she says. "The Bluebird has become part of the fabric of Nashville and really part of the process for artists and songwriters to get started here. When you first get in, you get out of your car or get off the bus and you've got to find a place where you can walk in and start playing. The Bluebird is one of those live music venues where the doors are always open."

———

When a brand is successful, opportunities to cash in on that success—opportunities that come from the outside in—should be

weighed against the brand's core values. That is easier said than done. Similarly, when a brand is faltering or changing hands, any opportunity to turn a profit can be difficult to turn down. Regardless of the financial circumstances, modern legacy builders like Kurland speak through action; that is how you build modern legacy from the inside out.

Under the NSAI and Wollam Nichols, The Bluebird Cafe remains true to its roots to this day because its leadership values long-term ambitions more than short-term profits. The Bluebird Cafe Concert Series in Sundance—which began under Kurland and features multiple events throughout the summer—continues more than 15 years later. Since Kurland's departure, The Bluebird's star has continued to rise, much like many of the legends who got their start on its stage. Today, The Bluebird sponsors and curates events around the world, such as the C2C: Country to Country festival in London, England. Most notably, in 2012, The Bluebird became a regular on-set location in the hit TV show *Nashville*.

"I couldn't be more thrilled with being part of [the show *Nashville*] and, in general, with the way The Bluebird is represented," says Kurland. "The Bluebird is a character in the show. And with all the crazy, dramatic things that happen [on the show], whenever they want to get back to the heart and the soul and the reason why people do this, they put a song in The Bluebird—and I love that." So do The Bluebird's loyal fans and performers.

Although the growing spotlight has resulted in perennially sold-out shows for the tiny space, the NSAI and Wollam Nichols have continued to cultivate the spirit of Kurland's Bluebird for the next generation to enjoy, keeping true to the brand culture Kurland passed forward and Wollam Nochols carries on. Proud of what The Bluebird continues to achieve, Kurland still counts herself among its regulars. After all, some shows are too good to miss.

Such was the case on a cool October evening in 2016 when Garth Brooks returned to play on the stage where he got his start in Nashville. Nearly 30 years since his Bluebird debut, Brooks is the bestselling solo artist in U.S. history, having sold more than 149 million albums, beating Elvis Presley

Clockwise from top: Founder of The Bluebird Cafe Amy Kurland with singer-songwriter David Crosby; Kurland (left), with songwriter Gary Burr and bartender Katy DiGiovanni; and Kurland (right) with songwriter Victoria Shaw.

Images courtesy of Amy Kurland

and second only to the Beatles in total album sales overall.[16] Yet there he sat before an audience not much bigger than the one at his first performance at The Bluebird three decades earlier. Once again, he got a standing ovation.

"Garth Brooks is a tremendous talent," says Kurland. "He didn't need The Bluebird to get famous. He needed to be seen in person in a setting where people were really listening."

Fortunately for country music audiences and artists alike, The Bluebird is still providing just that. Stop in the next time you pass through Music City. Kurland may not be there to greet you, but because of the modern legacy she passed forward—putting deeds before words and sticking to the brand's values—The Bluebird's doors are still open today.

In building your modern legacy, how can you find ways to show rather than tell?

Kurland built The Bluebird Cafe and passed it forward for the next generation to enjoy by staying focused on what she did best: providing a world-class listening room for country music singer-songwriters at every stage in their careers. When musicians suggested ways to improve the space, she acted on their advice. When larger audiences began packing the place, she made sure they adhered to the cafe's motto ("Shhh!"). When success afforded her the opportunity to host increasingly famous artists, she nevertheless saved space and time for up-and-coming musicians. Finally, when she decided to retire from the business she founded after more than 25 years of auditions and ovations, she ensured that she left

The Bluebird in the hands of people who would walk the talk just like her. Speaking through her actions, Kurland built her modern legacy by always behaving in the best interests of her brand.

Beliefs behaved become deeds. How do you align your beliefs and behaviors with your brand's best interests? Start by asking what "one thing" you do best. If your beliefs are in service of your one thing, they are more apt to become words to live by. If they are not, they're just words.

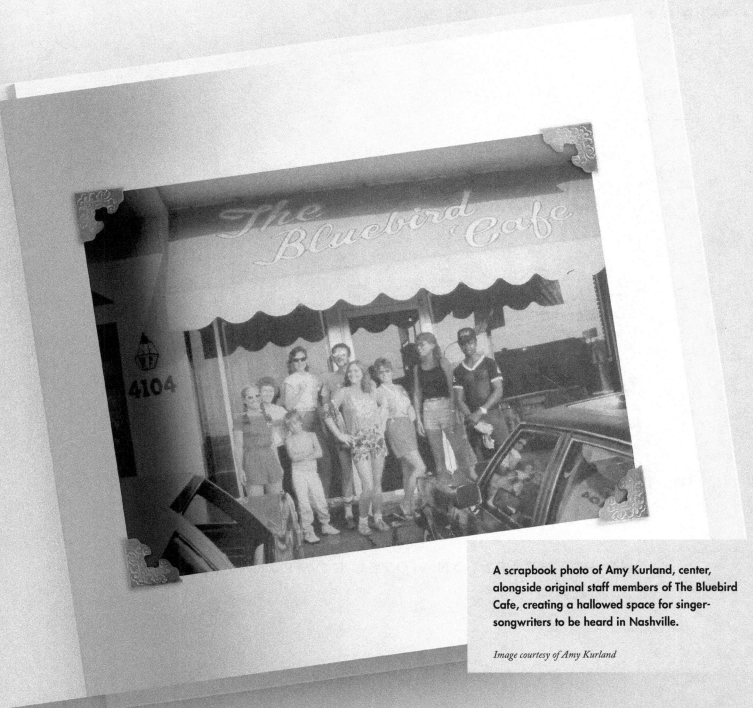

A scrapbook photo of Amy Kurland, center, alongside original staff members of The Bluebird Cafe, creating a hallowed space for singer-songwriters to be heard in Nashville.

Image courtesy of Amy Kurland

---

(1) **Your Culture Is Your Product**
THE HONEST COMPANY
Established 2012

(2) **Deeds, Not Words**
THE BLUEBIRD CAFE
Established 1982

(3) # Empower Your Believers

THE RITZ-CARLTON HOTEL COMPANY

Established 1983

THE RITZ-CARLTON, DUBAI, is a palatial resort situated on the broad white sands of Jumeirah Beach in the United Arab Emirates. Its low-slung suites with richly detailed Arabic and Mediterranean architectural accents eschew the soaring skyscrapers for which the city has become famous. Adjacent to the Emirates Golf Club and the JBR Walk, Jumeirah Beach is Dubai's only beachfront promenade of luxury retail boutiques and *al fresco* cafes. The Ritz-Carlton property there is designed to provide patrons with anything they could want in a luxury beachfront resort. Although The Ritz-Carlton prides itself on anticipating its guests' wishes, every now and then something new comes along.

One afternoon not too long ago, a 14-year-old boy in a wheelchair looked out on the clear blue waters of the Persian Gulf. Speaking wistfully to his family, he talked about swimming "in that beautiful ocean." The boy had never walked in his life, let alone swam.

Though the resort and the ocean were separated by about 200 meters of sand—making it impassable to anyone in a wheelchair—the staff heard about the boy's wish, and in a matter of hours the hotel engineer had built a wooden walkway leading to the surf. That same day, for the first time in his life, the young boy left his wheelchair on the beach and went swimming in the ocean.

This is what The Ritz-Carlton calls a "Wow" story: an example of generosity and anticipatory service that "creates a memory for someone that will last a lifetime." Hervé Humler, a founding member of the hotel brand and now the company's chairman emeritus, regularly shares Wow stories with his colleagues at the brand's headquarters. It's nothing new. In fact, sharing Wow stories like this is a daily practice at each of the company's 90-plus properties all over the world. By sharing these Wow stories, the brand's employees in turn inspire their colleagues to new heights of service.

"What I'm proudest of is that it's not about telling our employees they have to do it," Humler says. "Nobody told our hotel engineer in Dubai that he had to build a walkway. Instead, we have built a culture, and an ambience, in which employees want to do their job. And we, more importantly, have empowered our people to do so. Empower-

ment is a very powerful and meaningful ingredient. Our people want to make an active, not passive, contribution to be a real part of making something memorable."

Based on the number of Wow stories coming out of The Ritz-Carlton, Humler and his colleagues have struck on a winning formula for empowering their employees or, as the brand prefers to call them, "ladies and gentlemen."

———————

The Ritz-Carlton Hotel Company has long been lauded for setting the gold standard for anticipatory service, twice earning the Malcolm Baldrige National Quality Award presented by the president of the United States. In 2016, the company was named the top-ranking luxury hotel brand in North America for guest satisfaction by J.D. Power and Associates, receiving the highest score ever earned by any luxury brand in that category.[17]

Reflecting on the brand's enduring success, however, Humler doesn't focus solely on con-

ventional business measures such as RevPAR (revenue per available room). Nor does he dwell on survey-driven accolades like those noted above. Instead, Humler speaks passionately about the need for ongoing investment in the brand's strong internal culture by empowering employees to add to the brand's story.

"Our 40,000 ladies and gentlemen not only embrace the culture that has been passed down, but they also contribute to growing the culture every day," he says. "We are constantly opening hotels around the world. No matter how beautiful a building might be, it never has heart or soul until we animate it with our employees."

In an increasingly homogenized global economy in which computers answer most customer service calls and self-checkout lanes are increasingly common, The Ritz-Carlton has a refreshingly human approach to service. Everyone contributes, and Humler readily declares that his employees are more important than he is. In contrast, perhaps the biggest flaw in the way traditional organizations think about employee culture is the misconception that it can be maintained from the top down with corporate identity manuals and human resources training sessions alone. These methods amount to simply telling people to do something rather than empowering them. Internal culture is not a top-down arrangement; culture goes both ways. Engaged employees want to contribute in a meaningful way, not simply fall in line.

It's a lesson The Ritz-Carlton learned through experience.

"In the early 1980s and 1990s, we focused too literally on consistency," Humler recalls. "The fronts of The Ritz-Carlton hotels all looked the same. The inside of the hotels all looked the same. The bedrooms all looked the same." Similarly, the brand once expected guests at its restaurants to abide by a standard dress code. Both are examples of how the brand used to manage uniformity and appearance.

In recent years, however, the brand has grown away from this kind of top-down uniformity, allowing each property to express more of its own unique identity and recognizing that new generations of guests increasingly express success in contemporary, less formal attire.

"We were too formal and stuffy for some," Humler admits. "A few years ago, when people would come to our hotel in jeans, we would say, 'If you don't have a coat and tie, you're not going to have dinner with us.' But now, when they come in with flip-flops, we say, 'Good day and welcome!'"

"Invest in people. Give them the tools they need to contribute to your vision, mission and culture."

Ultimately, The Ritz-Carlton's evolving understanding of what it means to be a place for successful people is perhaps best expressed in the way the brand now empowers its employees to bring its

values to life each day. Just as no one told the hotel engineer in Dubai that he had to build a walkway, success at The Ritz-Carlton is not about literal compliance or conformity. Success comes from helping employees internalize the company's principles so that each employee can express them in his or her own unique way. When everyone understands a brand's ambition and has the same passion, brand values will find their way into the fabric of the internal culture. It's essentially weaving a living tapestry of modern legacy that everyone can appreciate and add to rather than simply comply with. It all comes back to empowerment, Humler says.

"Invest in people," he explains. "Give them the tools they need to contribute to your vision, mission, and culture."

Long celebrated for its service philosophy beyond the hotel industry, in 2000 The Ritz-Carlton opened its Leadership Center. The vision: Share what the company has learned about embracing a culture of service with brands in other industries. The results speak for themselves. Apple famously launched its Genius Bar after sending employees to the Leadership Center, and over the years brands in every imaginable industry—from automotive, energy, and finance to fitness, healthcare, technology, and more—have sent staff to learn how to inspire their employees. As a result, the impact of The Ritz-Carlton's empowerment philosophy can be felt all over the world.

Another method the brand uses to reinforce its values and empower its employees is through "Line-Ups," 15-minute meetings with employees. In contrast to staff meetings at some companies, which may happen once a week, month, or quarter, leaders at The Ritz-Carlton hold Line-Ups at the beginning of every shift—three times a day at all 90-plus locations around the world. Line-Ups are held even at the company's corporate headquarters, where Humler first started the tradition.

"You need to meet with your team for at least a few minutes every day," he says. "We cover the priorities for the day as well as reinforce our values. We talk about how we aim to treat our guests. We also share a Wow story"—like the story of the boy in the wheelchair who got to swim in the ocean.

Other Wow stories abound. There's the time a guest forgot his computer at the hotel and had to give a presentation later that day. A Ritz-Carlton employee found the laptop, boarded a flight, and delivered it in time for the event. And there's the time a little boy left behind a beloved toy giraffe at a hotel property. He was overjoyed and awestruck when the giraffe arrived in the mail days later, complete with a photo album of it kicking back by the pool, getting a massage at the spa, and enjoying the hotel's many amenities.

At the center of each Wow story are ladies and gentlemen—the brand's believers—and as their stories are celebrated internally, they empower other believers and inspire new stories for the world to see. It's a virtuous cycle in which The Ritz-Carlton aims to make sure all of its guests "get their memory's worth, not just their money's worth."

"Make the people around you the greatest evangelists of your brand," Humler advises. "People make you successful—so help people succeed."

In building your modern legacy, how can you hand the keys to your employees?

By encouraging its employees to let the brand's beliefs inspire their behaviors, The Ritz-Carlton sparks a positive feedback loop. Empowered employees create Wow stories, guests leave with lifelong memories, and the brand maintains an active channel of inspiring case studies that inspire other employees (resulting in more Wow stories, attracting more guests, and so on).

Do your employees buy into the same ideas you do? Do you trust them to make choices the way you do? If empowerment is about interpretation, not compliance, ask yourself what elements of your brand you could leave up to interpretation. Rather than reading from your brand's history, your employees might just help you add to it.

One of the gentlemen of The Ritz-Carlton living the culture of the brand by creating a memorable Wow story for a visiting young lady.

Image courtesy of The Ritz-Carlton Hotel Company

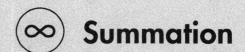 **Summation**

Although every modern legacy begins with ambitions, behaviors are the key to migrating from dreaming to doing. This is why we say that modern legacy building is behavioral: It requires enlisting others who share your ambitions and will work with you to achieve them. By harnessing shared beliefs to guide brand behaviors, The Honest Company, The Bluebird Cafe, and The Ritz-Carlton Hotel Company not only build strong, lasting brand cultures from the inside out, they also demonstrate how a long-term investment in brand culture enables faster short-term decision-making. In this way, their stories illustrate how a brand's cultural behavior can be a competitive advantage and an antidote to today's disease of short-term thinking.

At The Honest Company, principles preceded products. From their earliest meetings, Jessica Alba and Christopher Gavigan designed the company with culture at its heart. With the help of their cofounders, they have built a bonfire that keeps the brand's beliefs-driven culture scaling at a sustainable rate. Drawn by the light, consumers and profits have followed.

Amy Kurland's unwavering devotion to providing aspiring singer-songwriters with a place to be heard compelled her to limit The Bluebird Cafe's size. As a result, its prestige has only grown. Lacking experience in her industry, she learned on her feet, though her behaviors were always guided by her devotion to her brand.

And then there is Hervé Humler, The Ritz-Carlton Hotel Company's most ardent champion. By espousing a shared set of beliefs and empowering limitless unique behaviors, his brand's modern legacy has grown from one location in Boston to more than 90 flourishing hotels around the world. Whereas many brands still cling to the principle of control, Humler delegates, learning from his believers rather than simply telling them how to behave.

The Honest Company's bonfire, The Bluebird Cafe's devotion, and The Ritz-Carlton Hotel Company's believers all illustrate how long-term beliefs, when shared by way of strong brand cultures, inspire unique, imaginative behaviors. The results are easy to see: Rather than building their brands first from the outside in on posturing and attitude, these modern legacy builders start by bringing their inside out, ensuring that their beliefs guide their actions.

When your culture is your brand, an expectant mother can always trust the products you sell, though they may change. When you speak through deeds, not just words, the next potential country music superstar knows your door will be open when she steps off the bus in Nashville with nothing but her guitar. When you believe in your believers and empower them to act creatively, a hotel engineer might just be inspired to help a young wheelchair-bound boy swim in "that beautiful ocean" by building a bridge from dreaming to doing.

Modern legacy building is behavioral, and when you commit to building your brand by behaving in line with your long-term beliefs, short-term decisions become quicker and more intuitive.

THE LEGACY BUILDER'S
BALANCE SHEET

What's Your Why?

Most brands talk about what they make and how they make it. Not enough communicate why.

Fast Company's origin story is an excellent example of why brands should "start with why." The provocative instruction at the heart of author Simon Sinek's Golden Circle model, "starting with why" encourages brand leaders to reflect on *why* they do what they do. Although the other two questions—*how* a company conducts business and *what* functional products or services it sells—are more familiar, the why is the most important statement a company or leader can make to inspire others to rally around it and share in its central ambition. In the case of *Fast Company*, founding editors Bill Taylor and Alan Webber understood that the world of work and the competitive pace of global business were moving faster than others in their industry could keep up with.

In 1995, after successful careers as editors at the *Harvard Business Review*, Taylor and Webber set out to launch *Fast Company*. The clue to their "why" is still right there in the title of the magazine.

Just off a sabbatical in Japan, Webber was convinced that globally, business was changing—*fast*. The dawn of the Internet was revolutionizing the way businesses competed, people worked, and customers shopped. Webber and Taylor also saw that traditional U.S. media—including the business magazines and newspapers themselves—were missing those rapid changes entirely. Seeking to advocate for newer, faster, and better ways of competing (the brand's why), the cofounders named their new magazine *Fast Company*: a call to motivate leaders to perform at the speed of modern business.

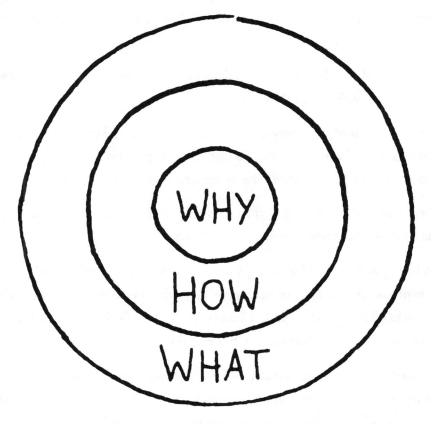

Know (W)hyself

More important than *what* you do or *how* you do it is *why*, the question at the core of author Simon Sinek's Golden Circle model. In 1995, Alan Webber saw a world changing faster than traditional media could keep up, so he cofounded a radically different kind of business magazine to cover it—*Fast Company*. What's your why? Look deep inside and to the origins of your brand. Your what and how (products and services) will resonate more with consumers and colleagues when the why behind them is authentic and meaningful.

Informed by their why, they came up with a clear, powerful manifesto (the brand's how) and printed that statement on the cover of the first issue: "Work is personal. Computing is social. Knowledge is power. Break the rules."

"The words on the cover of that first issue, including the *Fast Company* banner, were written to be nailed up on our office wall," says Webber.

Guided by an understanding of their why and how, the cofounders began looking for journalists and editors who shared their beliefs and could report on the changes taking place across multimedia platforms, most notably the magazine (the brand's what).

"Our elevator pitch was that we were going to create something that was a cross between the *Harvard Business Review* and *Rolling Stone*," says Webber.

Once they began hiring with traits like those in mind, a unique personality and character began to emerge. Irreverent and sharp, the brand's refreshing take on business generated a culture of attraction across the publishing industry. Applicants, eager to join the vanguard of a new era of business journalism, flooded the cofounders with résumés.

Readers loved it. Alongside its familiar established competitors, *Fast Company*'s unique perspective and style was an instant success. The company quickly rocketed from 100,000 launch issues to an estimated readership of more than 3 million and set a record as the fastest-growing business magazine in history.[18] *Fast Company* was literally a fast company.

Still thriving decades later, the *Fast Company* brand continues to reflect the very changes it reports on. By tapping into the why behind their brand and literally naming the magazine to indicate the rapidly evolving changes happening in business, *Fast Company* set the tone for how journalists everywhere report on the fast-paced, competitive digital era.

Can you identify your brand's why, how, and what—the concentric circles of the Golden Circle model? Can you distill your answers so that they are easy to share with others? To track your progress, take a couple of baseline measurements. How many qualified applicants do you get for every open position? How well do your employee tenure numbers stack up against the rest of your industry? When you build from the inside out and start with why, your culture of attraction will follow.

CHAPTER THREE

Let Outsiders In

"Treat your customers like they own you, because they do."

MARK CUBAN

Entrepreneur and Owner of the NBA's Dallas Mavericks[1]

FROM HIS FIRST JOB at the age of 12, enlisting his neighbors to buy garbage bags wholesale so that he could save up for a new pair of sneakers,[2] to his current role as a sage investor and advisor to fellow entrepreneurs on ABC's *Shark Tank*, Mark Cuban has always had a knack for engaging others, finding common interests, and building relationships.

For nearly 50 years, Cuban has been collaborating with partners, investors, and customers in countless businesses, working with them to build everything from multibillion-dollar software brands (he and a friend built Broadcast.com from scratch and sold it to Yahoo! in 1999)[3] to a professional basketball team (Cuban transformed the NBA's Dallas Mavericks into a championship team after buying the franchise at a low point and rallying the players and the fans around him).[4] Category after category—technology, publishing, sports, film, philanthropy, and numerous others—the iconic entrepreneur has a story to tell and is looking for audiences to help him share it.

Cuban's contribution to business and society goes beyond simply making money. Cuban makes waves. Whether he is stirring up players, fans, referees, and the media from his courtside seats at a Mavericks' game, sparking national debates about politics and philanthropy on Twitter, or unleashing new entrepreneurs, products, and businesses into the market through his investments on *Shark Tank*, he treats every conversation like the beginning of a cooperative campaign, looking to inspire or be inspired.

Now worth an estimated $3.3 billion,[5] Cuban is anything but an out-of-touch billionaire. Rather than building walls around his brands, he believes in treating customers as if they owned those brands. Rather than simply amassing money, he leverages his public profile to draw attention to philanthropic causes. A master in the art of sharing control and encouraging others to take part and add their voices, Cuban is at the vanguard of modern legacy's third transformation: from commanding and controlling customers to influencing social movements.

Transformation:

Nearsighted brand leaders hoard information and tell customers what to do, striving for category dominance and sales superiority.

Leaders with the modern legacy mindset consider their social influence and invite customers to help tell their story because sales follow saliency.

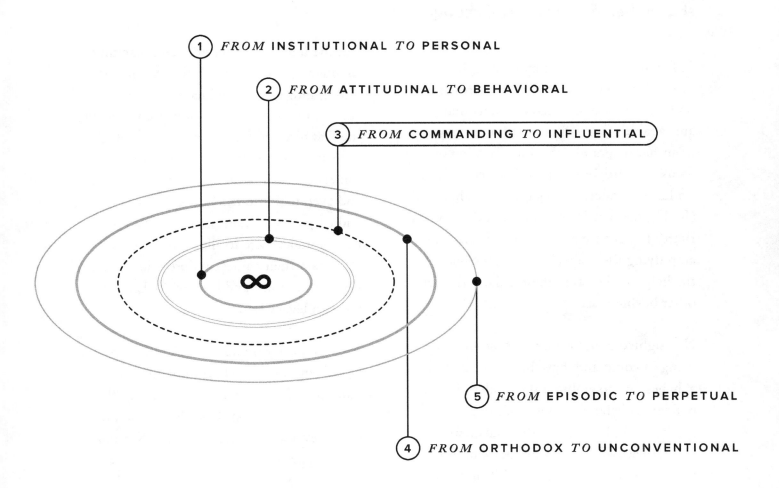

1. *FROM* INSTITUTIONAL *TO* PERSONAL

2. *FROM* ATTITUDINAL *TO* BEHAVIORAL

3. *FROM* COMMANDING *TO* INFLUENTIAL

5. *FROM* EPISODIC *TO* PERPETUAL

4. *FROM* ORTHODOX *TO* UNCONVENTIONAL

Could your personal ambitions and shared beliefs drive social change?

In Chapter 2, we began by looking inward, explaining how strong brand cultures are built around a shared set of beliefs that are capable of inspiring an infinite array of authentic brand behaviors. Turning our focus outward, in Chapter 3, we show how leaders at modern legacy brands such as (RED), the San Diego Zoo, and the It Gets Better Project are generating influence and amplifying their social impact by enlisting the help of advocates, the media, and even other businesses.

Nearsighted brand leaders, accustomed to being in command, have been understandably hesitant to embrace the modern legacy builder's collaborative approach to growing spheres of influence. Inviting outsiders in—rather than pushing influence out—represents an unprecedented shift in the ways in which brands engage their customers. Historically, even after radical changes in media and technology—from print to radio,

for example, or from radio to television—brands have always used media like a bullhorn, issuing commands for the customer to follow.

But the transformation from commanding to influential isn't just a shift in the media that brands use to conduct business; it's a shift in the way brands conduct business in the first place. With the rise of technologies such as the Internet and social media, customers can talk back, talk to one another, and even talk into the future. Informed and empowered, consumers are using their newfound leverage to align with brands that share their values and provide inspiration, community, and leadership. Enter the modern legacy brand.

Modern legacy brands trade in the currency of influence, not solely commands and repetition. Influence is at the heart of their business model, from how they launch to how they scale and create equity. Not only is this approach to generating influence more collaborative than the command model, it also is exponentially more effective at driving profound social change. At (RED), for example, cofounders Bono and Bobby

Shriver, along with refounder Deb Dugan, are rallying supporters by leading the quest for a world without AIDS. At the San Diego Zoo, refounder Ted Molter and others around the world are working to end extinction by sharing ideas and resources. And Dan Savage and Terry Miller's It Gets Better Project is reaching out to embattled lesbian, gay, bisexual, transgender, and queer (LGBTQ+) youth with the help of tens of thousands of online contributors. By allowing advocates to take a vested interest in their long-term personal ambitions and giving them a relevant insider stake as cocreators, the modern legacy builders in the pages ahead are generating influence and transforming their brands into enduring social movements.

① Effect Change

(RED)

Established 2006

② Share Your Secrets
THE SAN DIEGO ZOO
Established 1916

③ Enroll Consumers as Coauthors
THE IT GETS BETTER PROJECT
Established 2010

ON JUNE 5, 1981, the U.S. Centers for Disease Control and Prevention prepared a weekly bulletin concerning the unusual case of five young, recently healthy Los Angeles men who were suffering from a variety of unusual immune disorders. By the time the now infamous report was published, two of the men had died. Unknown to the world, the global HIV/AIDS epidemic had begun.

In the months and years that followed, HIV and AIDS spread unchecked throughout the world, killing tens of millions. Even as medical treatments began to appear in the West, the epidemic continued to plague Sub-Saharan Africa, where medicines were often in short supply and were prohibitively expensive. At the peak of the epidemic, roughly 2 million people were dying each year from AIDS-related illnesses. Three million were contracting the virus, including nearly 1,300 babies every day.

In 2002, the Global Fund to Fight AIDS, Tuberculosis and Malaria—a public-private partnership—was created to address the devastating toll on human life. At the outset, dozens of leading nations pledged billions of dollars, but private contributions were anemic in comparison. Four years in, although the public sector had pledged approximately $5 billion, private contributions amounted to just over $5 million. This funding imbalance threatened the Global Fund's public-private charter and threatened to impede vital public contributions.

With billions of dollars of public funds and millions of lives at stake, something had to be done to spur contributions from private companies. Quickly.

Enter Bono, U2's legendary front man, and Bobby Shriver, famed attorney, activist, and Kennedy scion, who came up with an idea to help channel private sector dollars to the Global Fund called (RED). Since 2006, (RED) has generated funding to help end AIDS, with a specific focus on eliminating mother-to-child transmission. Ambitious? Certainly. After all, who ever inspired profound, enduring change with a reasonable goal?

———————————

Meeting consumers' needs with good products at a good price is a good way to stay in business. This is not, however, an inspiring

> *"Companies now have to be innovative about how they approach social good in the same way they have to be innovative about new products."*

competitors have been up to in the most recent sales quarter. Instead, they ask questions such as "How will the world be forever different as a result of what I am doing?" and "What can I do that no one else has done before?"

(RED), for example, is not a typical charity. Although the goal was to persuade brands to contribute to the Global Fund, (RED) wasn't asking for handouts. Rather, the non-profit organization presented an innovative approach to philanthropy unlike anything else before it: entice famous brands to create (RED)-licensed products and donate a portion of the resulting proceeds to fight HIV/AIDS. The resulting capitalistic-philanthropic alchemy has surpassed all expectations.

"Prior to (RED), you had a select group like Newman's Own and Ben & Jerry's that were each doing their own initiative for good," recalls Deb Dugan, (RED)'s CEO since 2011. "(RED) believed that if it could tap into the marketing smarts of the brightest and best minds in its partner companies, it had a chance to present the issue in a non-earnest and fresh way. That would be good for companies and their sales and at the same time drive more money to the

path to driving transformative, lasting change. From the outset, (RED)'s cofounders, Bono and Shriver, understood that building a modern legacy isn't about maximizing shareholder value; it's about maximizing your cultural contribution. Leaders and brands like this aren't easily distracted by what their

AIDS fight while helping to keep the issue of AIDS at the top of the political agenda."

In practice, (RED)'s symbiotic formula for generating social influence works three ways: brands such as Apple and Gap draw customers' attention and drive sales by releasing limited edition (RED)-branded products with charity cachet; consumers have the opportunity to give and receive simultaneously, achieving a higher purpose with their purchases; and (RED) spreads an important message while sending the proceeds on to the Global Fund. It's a winning formula: sell more, influence more, and—most important—save lives.

Working toward this long-term goal is just one way the team at (RED) is building the brand's modern legacy. At the same time, (RED) is building that legacy on a day-to-day basis by inspiring more brands to do good, creating the kind of impact that can't always be measured with dollars and statistics. As evidence, Dugan points to changes in the ways in which corporate America now embraces philanthropy.

"Companies now have to be innovative about how they approach social good in the same

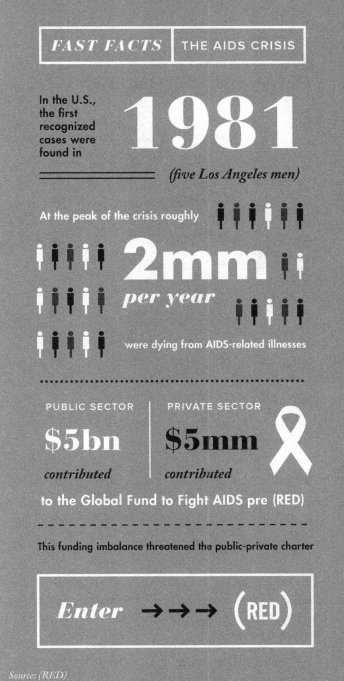

FAST FACTS | THE AIDS CRISIS

In the U.S., the first recognized cases were found in **1981**
(five Los Angeles men)

At the peak of the crisis roughly **2mm** *per year* were dying from AIDS-related illnesses

PUBLIC SECTOR **$5bn** *contributed* | PRIVATE SECTOR **$5mm** *contributed*

to the Global Fund to Fight AIDS pre (RED)

This funding imbalance threatened the public-private charter

Enter → → → (RED)

Source: (RED)

As part of its evolution from products into experiences, (RED) hired celebrated designer Jonathan Adler to create a themed suite, featuring artwork by Kelsey Montague, at the Andaz West Hollywood hotel. Debuting in March 2017, 30% of each stay in the suite is contributed to (RED)'s fight against AIDS.[6]

Images courtesy of (RED)

way they have to be innovative about new products," Dugan says. "This changes the definition of what it means to create shareholder value."

(RED)'s track record speaks for itself. Its first (RED)-branded products included those from American Express, Gap, Motorola, Converse, Giorgio Armani, and Apple. Since then, the charity has branched out from products into experiences with leading celebrities, including Matt Damon, Kim Kardashian, Tom Brady, Meryl Streep, and The Weeknd, among others. Other initiatives and events have generated millions more, including art and design auctions, an original U2 song released during the 2014 Super Bowl, and EAT (RED) SAVE LIVES, an initiative that lets restaurants, bars, and food trucks go (RED) for the month of June.

How has (RED) managed to stay relevant as media reports concerning HIV/AIDS have dwindled? Dugan says that capturing attention and inspiring action begins with identifying a "shared moment of interest," whether it is a product, an experience, or an emerging social media platform.

"(RED) needs to fish where the fish are to reach and inspire youth," she says. "Collectively, these young people are tuned in to what's happening around the world. We have to employ the technology of the current generation to give our audience the tools to get involved."

To do that, (RED) strives to be a cultural curator in all that it does, always in search of new opportunities. On World AIDS Day 2009, for example, (RED) teamed with Twitter to turn the online news and social networking site the color red every time someone used the hashtag #RED.[7] (RED)'s social media strategy has been so effective, in fact, that it was the first not-for-profit to reach 1 million followers on both Twitter and Facebook. More recently, (RED) has been working on Snapchat and Instagram to create (RED) filters and video content—all inspired by "shared moments of interest." Though (RED) has never changed its message, it is always looking for new ways to express that message so that the brand can continue to effect change.

Notably, (RED)'s impressive list of social media firsts has myriad other indirect benefits beyond fund-raising.

"The millennial generation is so engaged with brands that stand for good," says Dugan. "They will switch a brand preference to support a cause they care about, they will advocate for the brands they believe in on their social channels, and most will even take a cut in pay to work at a socially responsible company that aligns with their personal values. Those younger than 18, the up-and-coming Gen Z, are even more idealistic."

By fishing where the fish are, even as the tides of culture and technology change unpredictably, (RED) is changing the way people think about philanthropy, a traditionally risk-averse discipline. Although (RED)'s innovative methods don't always come off as planned (Dugan counts a one-off film project among the charity's teachable moments), the brand's willingness to take chances, fail, and "learn fast" enables it to reach new audiences.

"We don't just wind up in the latest and emerging channels—we wind up doing something innovative in those channels," says Dugan. "Whatever we do, we aim to be big."

Nearly 12 years into its ambitious world-changing mission to generate influence, (RED) is still grabbing headlines and making a profound social impact. To date, the organization has raised more than half a billion dollars for the Global Fund, affecting the lives of more than 100 million people. In the process, the number of children born with HIV each day has been cut by more than two-thirds. By 2020, the global health organizations are aiming to virtually eliminate mother-to-child transmission of the virus. By 2030, experts say the world could reach the end of AIDS as a global pandemic.

"It's maybe a funny way to look at it, but part of (RED)'s legacy is that it should be so successful that we put ourselves out of business," says Dugan.

(RED)'s story is not just one of harnessing ambition but also one of innovatively leveraging capitalism and consumer-driven altruism to achieve the kind of global change that neither companies nor consumers could effect on their own. To do this, the brand stays fascinated with media and technology, studying what motivates the next generation. To drive influence, keep partner brands engaged, and keep customers playing key roles, (RED) consistently gives them new platforms to work with.

Working to end the transmission of HIV/AIDS remains a profound ambition, but with the help of social influence, (RED) is working to change the way the world looks at solving big problems. Even if (RED) succeeds at putting itself out of business, its modern legacy will live on as similar organizations carry on the model it pioneered.

Refounder Deb Dugan, CEO, (RED).

Image courtesy of (RED)

In building your modern legacy, how might you apply the concept of addition by subtraction to effect change?

Imagine if the purpose of your brand was not to add something to the world—such as a product, service, or experience—but to take something away. What if success meant counting down, not up? (RED)'s long-term ambition is motivated by precisely that: addition through subtraction. By decreasing the number of children born with AIDS, (RED) is making the world a better place.

Notably, although (RED) measures success by what it subtracts from the world, its strategy for addition by subtraction relies on inspiring as many brands and customers as possible to help the cause. The more supporters (RED) can bring together—and the more impassioned those supporters become as a result of

(RED)'s influence—the fewer children will be born with AIDS.

Although few organizations have so weighty an ambition, all could learn something from (RED)'s strategic approach to influencing audiences and effecting change. Rather than focusing on what your brand adds to the world, consider what it might take away. Do your products, services, or experiences improve your customers' lives by eliminating anything? Applying the concept of addition through subtraction, how would you rally more advocates to your brand in the spirit of effecting positive change?

Like (RED), our next modern legacy builder is devoted to letting outsiders in, in the name of stopping a global crisis.

Deb Dugan rallying supporters on World AIDS Day 2015 during the BUILD Series at AOL Studios In New York.

Desiree Navarro/Getty Images

1 **Effect Change**
(RED)
Established 2006

2 # Share Your Secrets

THE SAN DIEGO ZOO

Established 1916

3 **Enroll Consumers as Coauthors**
THE IT GETS BETTER PROJECT
Established 2010

DEEP IN THE ALAKAI SWAMP in the heart of the Hawaiian island of Kauai, Jeremy Hodges watches intently as his team gingerly hoists a 40-foot ladder within inches of a tiny bird's nest tucked high in the branches overhead. A researcher with San Diego Zoo Global's Hawaii Endangered Bird Conservation Program, Hodges and his colleagues have hiked miles to reach this remote site, home to the endangered Hawaiian honeycreeper.[8] With their eyes fixed on the nest, the team's efforts in the next few minutes will determine whether the trek through the rain forest and bogs was worth the day's journey.

Once abundant in the Hawaiian Islands, honeycreepers have been decimated by habitat loss, avian malaria, predation by nonnative mammals, and competition from nonnative birds. Of the 51 species of honeycreeper historically native to the area, fewer than half still exist. Collecting two of the fragile eggs—each weighing little more than an M&M—Hodges's team immediately places them in an incubation carrier and transports them to a waiting helicopter. The mother bird will soon lay more eggs, and—with time, care, and a little luck—the eggs incubated by the research team will hatch and the birds will thrive in a protected wildlife area, allowing the honeycreeper's numbers to increase.

Welcome to the zoological way to build a modern legacy, in which conservation researchers, animal care experts, and veterinarians leave the San Diego Zoo environment and travel to the far corners of the globe to share their experience and resources in the name of protecting endangered plants and animals in their natural habitats. Thanks to the San Diego Zoo Institute for Conservation Research, dozens of teams like Hodges's are deployed across more than 40 countries around the world, working with local researchers to save hundreds of species from extinction. Requiring the coordinated efforts of some 200 scientists and millions of dollars in annual funding, San Diego Zoo Global is the largest zoo-based multidisciplinary research effort in the world. Its ethos for spending so much time and money sharing its secrets is as generous as it is ominous: It has no desire to be the last zoo standing.

"We have boots on the ground, we have folks in laboratories, we have the keepers and caregivers here," says Ted Molter, San Diego

San Diego Zoo Global, the zoo's umbrella organization, works to save species such as the Hawaiian honeycreeper.

©San Diego Zoo Global

Zoo Global's chief marketing officer and the person responsible for championing the zoo's many conservation projects, such as the one involving Hodges and the Hawaiian honeycreepers. "We're really trying to foster an awareness of how we're going to take care of not just wildlife *in* the zoo but wildlife *out* of the zoo."

Founded in 1916, the San Diego Zoo is known the world over as a leader in its field. Credited with pioneering open-air, cageless animal environments designed to recreate natural habitats, it also has one of the largest and most loyal zoological membership groups in the world, representing more than 500,000 members, donors, and advocates, including 130,000 children.

For decades, the San Diego Zoo has been sending its experts all over the world in an effort to end extinction. In service of this grand ambition, the zoo has been sharing its cutting-edge resources and century of insti- tutional knowledge with other zoos, universities, and conservationists. Somehow it is working. Despite the formidable challenges, experts from San Diego Zoo Global have helped reintroduce some 30 species, including the California condor and the Arabian oryx. In conjunction with its conservation efforts, the zoo maintains a "Frozen Zoo" with some 10,000 living cell cultures, sperm, and embryos. The Frozen Zoo is even preserving the DNA of an extinct species—the po'ouli, another Hawaiian bird—in the hope that advances in science will allow the zoo or one of its many research partners to bring the po'ouli back to life one day. Talk about building a modern legacy by bringing the past forward!

"If it works here and it contributes to the welfare of the animals that we're responsible for, we don't want to hide these concepts," explains Molter. "We want to share them."

In fact, San Diego Zoo Global's modern legacy of sharing is rooted long ago in the days before it was founded, with the opening of the Panama Canal in 1914. As the first port of call for ships traveling to the West Coast, San Diego hosted the 1915 Panama–California Exposition to share everything the port city had to offer with the world. Years in construction, the exposition included an amusement park, a 250-foot replica of the Panama Canal, an exhibit populated by seven Native American tribes, and some 2 million plants. Organizers took particular pride in an exotic animal exhibit featuring animals from all over the world. As "Colonel" D. C. Collier, one of the organizers of the exposition, said at the time, "The purpose of the Panama–California Exposition is to illustrate the progress and possibility of the human race, not for the exposition only, but for a permanent contribution to the world's progress."[9] It was a prescient declaration, at least as far as the exotic animal exhibit was concerned.

As attendance at San Diego's exposition dwindled after a couple years, local physician Harry M. Wegeforth founded the Zoological Society of San Diego to give the collection of exotic animals a permanent home. Whereas other zoos at the time used cages and organized animals in taxonomic groups (much like photos in a textbook), Wegeforth created wire-free environments circled by moats, which became methods that other zoos soon mimicked.

By 1975, with extinction on the rise, the San Diego Zoo drew on its longstanding tradition of innovation to launch its own department devoted to protecting endangered species. Although the zoo had always led by example to make a social impact, fighting extinction required sharing secrets in real time all over the world. Now more than 40 years in development, the project is the result of unprecedented levels of coordination among zoos, academic institutions, governmental agencies, and nonprofits everywhere.

"There's probably not a week that goes by that we don't have what we refer to as a 'visiting colleague,'" says Molter. In fact, the zoo opens its doors to so many outside researchers that its leadership may not even know who is on campus at any given time.

"At our executive meetings every week we say, 'Who's got out-of-town guests? Come and see us,'" he says. "They range from everywhere around the world."

Beyond hosting experts from other facilities, the zoo sends specialists from various disciplines to work alongside researchers anywhere species are in danger, such as the Alakai Swamp on Kauai. Molter says that sharing the zoo's knowledge and expertise is one of the main reasons the zoo has remained at the top of its field.

"We want to be part of a flourishing environment of good-quality zoos that have animal welfare at the forefront," Molter says. "When we learn something or we experience something that will allow us to take even better care of the animals, we want to make sure our colleagues everywhere know about it."

The zoo's wildly successful giant panda breeding program stands as an inspiring example of how sharing insights with others in the same field can pay unexpected dividends.

"Our colleagues in China were very concerned about the future of pandas," says Molter. The Chinese "were not having a great deal of success in panda mating and reproduction," he explains, despite creating wildlife preserves and working intensely to understand the endangered species' breeding patterns.

Whereas other zoos had tried to breed the animals during short-term borrowing programs, in the late 1990s, the San Diego Zoo made an initial 12-year commitment to the species, one that continues to this day. Seeking to understand giant pandas "down to the molecular level," zoo researchers monitored behavior patterns and hormones, ultimately cracking a long-elusive code and sharing what they learned with their Chinese counterparts.

"We've been very successful in bringing pandas here to San Diego, but our success is even bigger in the sense that what we learned was then shared with our Chinese colleagues," Molter says. "They've had seasons where they've had a couple dozen pandas born at their reserves. Now I'm happy to say that it's been so successful that they are considering putting pandas back into habitats in China, something that wasn't expected to occur for probably another 20 years."

Complex coordination with others in the field was also key to the zoo's success with the California condor, a species that essentially was given up for lost. In 1987, with only 22 of the birds left on Earth, the San Diego Zoo and partners such as the U.S.

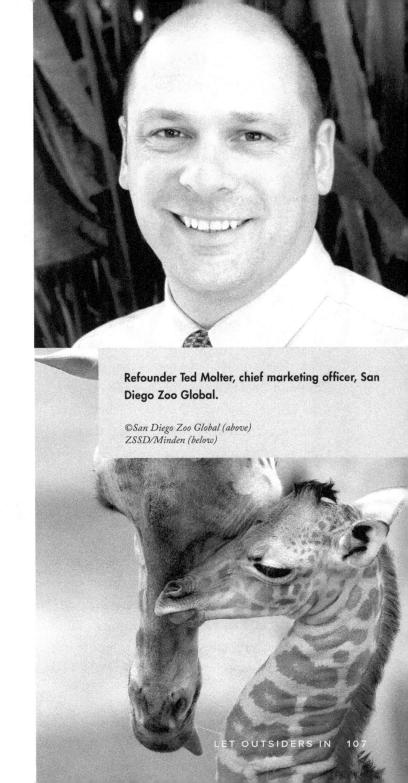

Refounder Ted Molter, chief marketing officer, San Diego Zoo Global.

©San Diego Zoo Global (above)
ZSSD/Minden (below)

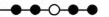

Fish and Wildlife Service captured all the remaining condors and began breeding them in captivity. Though successfully breeding the birds was the first step, Molter says that feeding, monitoring, and supporting the birds in the wild is why the species' numbers have rebounded to more than 450 birds in just 30 years.

"Half of [the condors] are outside the zoological facilities, flying free in the wild, but they are still monitored and they're still provided for," he says. "They eat carrion and carcasses, and we have teams that put carcasses in locations where they can observe the birds. Now we're at a point where there are enough condors out there that they're able to reproduce on their own. It's because we're now aware of the challenges in their environment, the challenges that humans impose on them, and what we can do to help them maintain their population going forward. It's not just, 'Hey, we had a baby hatch,' or 'We're creating an optimal condition in which these animals can mate and reproduce.' That's just the beginning of a very, very long tale and commitment to helping the species thrive in the wild."

Another of the zoo's ongoing commitments is educating children. The zoo is famous for designing exhibits, tours, and educational programs for kids and offers free admission to children during the month of October. Like the research and talent it shares with others in the industry, Molter says that sharing a love of animals with the next generation is key to the survival of animals everywhere.

"The future of the zoo and the future of wildlife is going to be about children," Molter says. "Activating and engaging young minds will be what makes a difference going forward. I put my faith in their ability to really think about these things and come up with solutions to challenges we're just starting to tackle."

Fortunately, the cultural impact the zoo is making today will help ensure that the next generation can continue the fight to end extinction. Recently, for example, the zoo has worked to reintroduce more endangered species of birds into the islands of Hawaii. The team has successfully managed sustainable populations of a number of species under human care and is taking the next significant step in their recovery.

In building your modern legacy, what could you beg, borrow, and share for the betterment of all?

As no single organization can end global extinction on its own, the San Diego Zoo shares its research and leverages its relationships to broaden its influence and social impact far beyond what it could accomplish on its own. Although the zoo is famous for supporting its colleagues in the field by contributing its own resources, it is also willing to ask for help and rely on others' expertise when necessary. The positive influence goes both ways.

Rather than hoarding your secrets, how could you demonstrate leadership by sharing them? What could you create that others might take and apply in your name? After all, no one gets credit for ideas that are never shared.

As a result of what the San Diego Zoo has learned and shared since the late 1990s, efforts to return the giant panda to natural habitats are nearly 20 years ahead of schedule.

©San Diego Zoo Global

1 **Effect Change**
(RED)
Established 2006

2 **Share Your Secrets**
THE SAN DIEGO ZOO
Established 1916

3 # Enroll Consumers as Coauthors

THE IT GETS BETTER PROJECT

Established 2010

BY THE AGE OF 15, Billy Lucas had been tormented by his peers for years because they perceived him to be gay. Just days before his suicide in September 2010, Billy's mother, Ann Lucas, recalled speaking to him about what it felt like to be relentlessly harassed and taunted.

"He told me 'Mom, you don't know what it's like to walk down the halls of school and be afraid of who's going to hit you, who's going to kick you.'"[10]

Upon hearing of Lucas's death, Dan Savage, the internationally syndicated writer and relationship columnist, was heartbroken and outraged.

"These kids told him he was a faggot," Savage recalls. "They embarrassed him. And they successfully encouraged him to kill himself."

Worse, the bullying continued online even after Billy's death.

"These same kids went to Billy's Facebook memorial page, a page set up by his family, and called him a faggot one more time,"

Savage remembers. "They said they were glad that he was dead. They said it in front of his parents. I was furious about it."

Savage responded with a "rageful post" of his own. Others spoke up, too, including one commenter who said, "I wish I had known you, Billy, and had been able to tell you that things get better. Rest in peace."

"That comment just stuck in my head," says Savage. "Because things do get better."

Despite being a successful author with millions of readers, Savage was frustrated by the traditional barriers to reaching out to teens like Billy. Schools rarely invite LGBTQ+ leaders to speak to teenage students, and some traditional community leaders are bigots and bullies themselves.

"Queer kids need LGBTQ+ adults to help put this period of their lives into perspective; they are in need of the sorts of strategies, tools, and coping mechanisms that we all use to get through this," says Savage. "But we can't talk to them. We never get permission to talk to them. Except we now live in the Twitter/Facebook/YouTube era."

Since 2010, the It Gets Better Project has inspired more than 60,000 videos and more than 60 million views.

Images courtesy of the It Gets Better Project

Inspired by the access created through social media, Savage and his partner, Terry Miller, launched the It Gets Better Project, posting encouraging video testimonials about their own experiences to reach bullied LGBTQ+ teens.

"I made the first video and launched the project," Savage recalls. "It felt grand and ambitious. But mostly, when we posted our one video, we just hoped that we wouldn't fall down flat on our faces."

Setting out to enlist the public's help, Savage and Miller asked people to contribute videos of their own. The response was overwhelming. Though Savage and Miller set an initial goal of collecting as many as 100 testimonials, they were inundated with thousands of videos in the very first week.

"There was a lot of gasoline on the ground," says Savage. "And we had a match."

In every modern legacy, there's a time to lead by example and a time to step out of the way.

Not long ago, the idea of letting outsiders control a brand's message would have given corporate executives fits. Today, it's practically a badge of honor. Whether it's a mainstream logo hijacked by a graffiti artist, a product creatively repurposed by a YouTube star, or customers voting to steer the philanthropic efforts of their favorite company, engaged advocates are contributing to brand strategy and blurring the traditional lines of marketing in new ways every day. Along the way, they are revolutionizing the ways messages are shared and markets are influenced.

Some organizations, such as the It Gets Better Project, are designed to be consumer-powered from the start. By reflecting on their own experiences being bullied, LGBTQ+ adults contributing to It Gets Better have been able to sidestep the conventions of the traditional media and conventional outreach groups by directly imparting their wisdom to young LGBTQ+ kids online. Going on eight years later, the movement has inspired more than 60,000 videos and more than 60 million views, including videos from President Barack Obama and the cast of NBC's *The Office*, as well as a bestselling book, a program on MTV, a comic book collaboration, and an online docuseries.

Indeed, the It Gets Better Project shows why some of the most resonant ideas, hacks, and viral inspirations come from consumers themselves: Free, spontaneous, and authentic, consumer-generated content is more readily shared and received than are most brand messages. Meanwhile, by enrolling customers as coauthors and allowing them to play an active role in guiding the narrative, these modern legacy builders are tapping deep reservoirs of consumer insight while simultaneously transforming everyday customers into long-term believers and advocates.

Of course, as an advocacy group based on video contributions, the It Gets Better Project had to enroll consumers as coauthors to thrive, but so does every organization. In today's short-term economy, any brand that hopes to drive lasting change, whether it is a consumer-packaged goods brand, a nonprofit, a university, or a political campaign, must be an advocacy brand. Although Savage is the first to say that the movement would have been a success if just one life had been saved, its influence on popular culture has been profound.

"For so long, we had culturally lived in denial of the existence of such a thing as LGBTQ+ children," he says. "Our culture wanted us to pretend that LGBTQ+ adults were fully formed in gay bars at the age of 21. Even when kids were coming out at an increasingly younger age, we had culturally given parents, teachers, and preachers the implied right to inflict suffering upon them."

As a result of organizations such as the It Gets Better Project, Savage says there has been a cultural reckoning. Empowered by a virtuous social cycle, the LGBTQ+ community is using It Gets Better to drive the kind of lasting cultural change that, once accomplished, cannot be reversed.

"We turned the contemporary culture in our favor," he says. "It Gets Better forced our culture to face up to the existence of LGBTQ+ kids."

———————

The key to the ongoing success of the It Gets Better Project has been its ability to

> "*[We] took away the inhibitions of people who wanted to make a difference, and who did not have permission to do so in the past.*"

enlist the help of its viewers, inspiring them to return to the site and contribute their own stories years later. In the years since the movement was founded, many of the young men and women who once came to it as teen viewers in need of perspective are now visiting the site as contributors, sharing their own inspiring videos with the next generation of LGBTQ+ youth.

Cofounder Dan Savage, the It Gets Better Project.

Image courtesy of the It Gets Better Project

"For us, the best advocates for the future of It Gets Better are those kids who are in their midtwenties now but who were in their midteens when the project got started and gained momentum," Savage says. "[We] took away the inhibitions of people who wanted to make a difference, and who did not have permission to do so in the past. We took the painful memories of LGBTQ+ adults and weaponized them in a wonderful way: turning them into a battering ram that they could use to break down a door and save a kid's life."

Beyond providing the movement with a steady stream of new content, the ability to enroll customers as coauthors has allowed it to sidestep existing barriers to reaching LGBTQ+ teens. Some of these challenges come from places one might expect: conservative groups, for example, such as the Family Research Council.

"It's not surprising that those groups would freak out because we were now talking directly to their kids," says Savage. "We are trying to save their kids from them!"

Other barriers to influence, however, came as a surprise. In particular, Savage points to

groups within the LGBTQ+ community that were bothered by how quickly and unconventionally the movement mobilized audiences and influenced culture. Some of the friendly fire came from LGBTQ+ groups that said the It Gets Better Project should have built a coalition before it launched.

"There are people out there who believe that they should be the gatekeepers for what is done and said by queer people about queer shit," he says. "I just went ahead and did this on my own—as if people aren't allowed to just do things on their own these days. And that is something that drove queer activists and queer organizations crazy."

Other LGBTQ+ groups said the It Gets Better Project wasn't doing enough to drive change.

"[They said] the project was too passive," he says. "[That we were] telling people to wait and not do anything, and things will get better all on their own."

Savage says such criticisms are uninformed.

"If you watch any of the videos, just one video, you'll see that it's people talking about what they did to help their situation get better," he says. "There is one video I particularly love that was posted by someone who would have been a senior in high school but was instead a freshman in college. In the video, the man explains that he got his GED and skipped senior year to get out of his high school, where he was getting brutalized. He was sharing how he made things better for himself."

Ultimately, opponents and naysayers aside, the It Gets Better Project's influential modern legacy speaks for itself. Literally.

"Even if we had only gotten 10 videos, even if the It Gets Better Project only saved one life, it would have been a tremendous success," says Savage. "That said, I hear from kids and parents all the time, constantly telling me that the project helped to save a life."

In what initially started out as just a few voices, the It Gets Better Project is now a social movement. By enlisting the help of a community eager for change, It Gets Better has empowered audience members to add their own voices. Through those voices, Savage, Miller, and the It Gets Better Project are driving social change and building a modern legacy far more influential than anything they could have imagined achieving on their own.

ZUMA Press, Inc./Alamy

In building your modern legacy, how could you make a durable difference by enrolling consumers as coauthors?

Although the idea of galvanizing popular culture may sound overwhelming, the strategy for generating influence behind the It Gets Better Project is actually quite simple: You don't have to write your brand's entire life story from beginning to end. You just have to persuade your consumers to help write it with you.

The hook? Ask your audience members for something doable, such as making a video and posting it to the Internet. After that, draw them in by showing some results. Beyond view counts, likes, and comments on specific videos, the It Gets Better Project demonstrates its success in the form of celebrity testimonials, spin-off projects such as the

docuseries *It Got Better*, and awards, including an Emmy for "creatively and powerfully utilizing the media to educate and inspire." Of course, these accolades only support the greatest evidence of the It Gets Better Project's success: the number of lives it has saved.

The more people love something, the more they're likely to add their voices and participate in a social movement. What's your cause? Who are your advocates? Finally, what could you do to actively enroll your advocates as coauthors? Once people see how their contributions can make a difference, they'll want to play a role.

IT GETS BETTER PRO

WWW

The It Gets Better Project, initially created as a space where online contributors could post video testimonials, is now a widespread social movement.

Lee Snider/Alamy

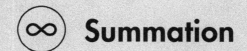 **Summation**

(RED), the San Diego Zoo, and the It Gets Better Project are all working to solve problems by leveraging social influence. Since they are nonprofits, the results these brands have achieved are all the more impressive because of the absence of standard market incentives such as discounts, dividends, and bonuses. Armed with long-term personal ambitions and strong beliefs and behaviors, each has managed to change the world in ways that many thought were impossible: striving to create a generation without AIDS, fighting to end extinction, and saving the lives of isolated LGBTQ+ teens. Notably, the tools and tactics these brands have employed to achieve such results are applicable to all modern legacy builders, nonprofit or otherwise.

Bono, Bobby Shriver, and Deb Dugan at (RED) effect change by incorporating the interests of brands and consumers in the name of adding to the world by subtracting something from it, namely, the transmission of AIDS from mothers to children. In the end, companies, customers, and communities all win. And when every party involved benefits, influence spreads.

The San Diego Zoo shares its secrets in the fight to end extinction because, in the words of Ted Molter, it doesn't want to be the last zoo standing. In the age of influence, this trend isn't limited to zoos. No matter what the industry, brands are forever cobranding, cooperating, and co-opting one another's best practices. Secrets are always being shared, borrowed, and bartered. Ultimately, lessons are useful only when they are shared.

Dan Savage and Terry Miller's It Gets Better Project taps into the influential power of social media by connecting with LGBTQ+ youth online and enrolling them as coauthors. Despite deeply entrenched social and cultural barriers, the movement's influence continues to spread. Any brand seeking to do the same has these universal tools at its disposal.

As the leaders at (RED), the San Diego Zoo, and the It Gets Better Project show so well, modern legacies are built with social influence—by letting outsiders in—not just sales superiority or category dominance. Each of the lessons they shared about building modern legacy with influence is inherently about being collaborative. Through effecting change, sharing secrets, and enrolling consumers as coauthors, these legacies in the making are finding ways to influence audiences and cause change reactions all over the world.

THE LEGACY BUILDER'S BALANCE SHEET

Pollinating a Culture of Influence

Like a queen bee in a hive, Mikaila Ulmer's long-term ambition is to build brands that motivate participation in a shared cause and unite others to create a meaningful change in the world. Though she just turned 13 in 2017, her dreams are already taking flight. *Time* magazine named Ulmer one of the "30 Most Influential Teens" of the year[11] and the National Retail Foundation included her among the "Top 25 People Shaping Retail's Future."[12]

A social entrepreneur since the age of four, Ulmer built her first brand, BeeSweet Lemonade, as a constructive response to being stung by two bees in the same week. Her goal: to raise awareness about the critical role bee species, many of which face extinction, play in the food chain. Success came quickly, and it wasn't long before BeeSweet Lemonade appeared on the reality TV show *Shark Tank*, where it landed a $60,000 investment. By the time BeeSweet was reaching shelves at select Whole Foods Markets, however, Ulmer had received a letter in the mail from a lawyer. Unknown to her, the name BeeSweet already belonged to another brand. The trademark law was clear, and Ulmer had to give up her brand.

Heartbroken but determined, the young social entrepreneur remained focused on her long-term personal ambition: creating a more bee-friendly world. As difficult as it was to give up the brand name, after some brainstorming with friends, her reimagined brand—Me & the Bees Lemonade— was born. Just like her first brand, this one generated immediate buzz.

When Barack and Michelle Obama learned of Ulmer's story, they invited her to a White House event. *Good Morning America* took part too, giving her an opportunity to publicly launch her

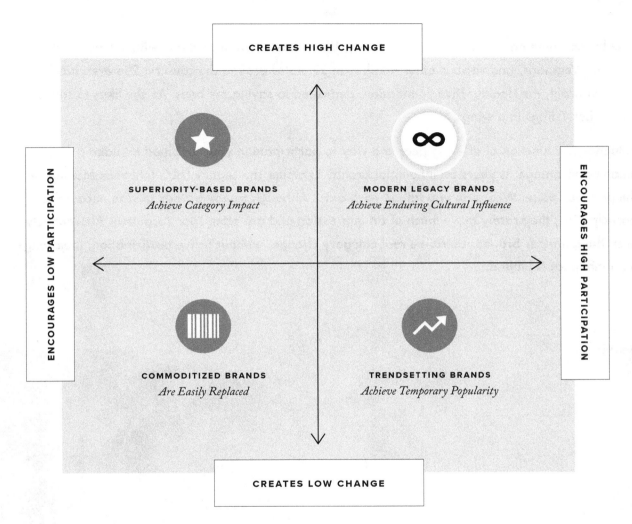

CREATES HIGH CHANGE

ENCOURAGES LOW PARTICIPATION

ENCOURAGES HIGH PARTICIPATION

SUPERIORITY-BASED BRANDS
Achieve Category Impact

MODERN LEGACY BRANDS
Achieve Enduring Cultural Influence

COMMODITIZED BRANDS
Are Easily Replaced

TRENDSETTING BRANDS
Achieve Temporary Popularity

CREATES LOW CHANGE

Spread the Buzz

The Legacy Lab's Influence Monitor illustrates how consumer engagement in the name of meaningful change creates a lasting impact on the world. By rallying advocates to save the bees, a critical link in our food chain, social entrepreneur Mikaila Ulmer is building Me & the Bees Lemonade and the Healthy Hive Foundation into inspiring brands with enduring cultural influence. Is yours a trendsetting, superiority-based, or commoditized brand, or are you pursuing long-term influence?

Source: The Legacy Lab

new brand name on national television. Today, Ulmer has distribution deals with Whole Foods Market, Wegmans, and various other retailers in 27 states around the country. She even has her own nonprofit, the Healthy Hive Foundation, dedicated to saving the bees. As she likes to say, she turned her "stings into wings."

Influence is a function of offering people a way to participate in your ambition to make a meaningful change. Is yours an influential brand? Examine The Legacy Lab's Influence Monitor on the previous page. Where do you fall on each axis? Although trendy brands tend to encourage participation, they rarely leave much of an impression and are often soon forgotten. Alternatively, even though other brands contribute real category change, without active participation, their long-term influence is limited.

Founder and CEO, Mikaila Ulmer, Me & the Bees Lemonade and the Healthy Hive Foundation.

Sandra Ramos/Courtesy of Me & the Bees Lemonade

Ulmer's long-term ambition is to create an impact so influential that both she and Me & the Bees Lemonade will leave a lasting impression on the world. In the interest of building a lasting brand through social impact and cultural influence, what can you do to inspire consumer engagement around a meaningful cause? Once you've plotted your brand on the monitor, ask how you might boost your influential position by rallying customers to your cause, letting outsiders in, and generating even greater change. The more inspiring your call to action, the more powerful your impact, and the more lasting the impression your brand will create.

CHAPTER FOUR

Invent Your Own Game

"If you decide that you're going to do only the things you know are going to work, you're going to leave a lot of opportunity on the table."

| JEFF BEZOS |

Founder, President, Chairman, and
Chief Executive Officer, Amazon[1]

IN 1982, after being named the valedictorian at his high school, Jeff Bezos gave an interview to the *Miami Herald*. Asked about his ambitions, the 18-year-old Bezos told the reporter he wanted to "build space hotels, amusement parks, yachts and colonies for two or three million people orbiting around the Earth."[2] Crazy, right?

A born disrupter, Bezos has made an art of turning crazy long-term ambitions into reality throughout his career. Not only did he leave his comfortable job at a New York hedge fund in 1994 to work out of his garage launching an online bookselling website called Amazon[3]—now a $500 billion brand[4] and one of the world's largest retailers[5]—Bezos also found time to launch Blue Origin, one of several private spaceflight companies competing to make his childhood dream of space tourism a reality.[6] Oh, and he also wants to deliver your groceries by drone from warehouses floating in the sky.[7]

Where most companies rely on the status quo and develop playbooks around it, Bezos has redefined entire industries—such as publishing, shipping, and retail—by finding creative solutions to problems everyone else takes for granted. One of the principles behind his success is his preference for learning by experimentation—what science fiction author Ray Bradbury called jumping off a cliff and building your wings on the way down—rather than try-

ing to avoid every error and becoming passive.[8] In fact, Bezos encourages his leadership, who as of 2017 manage Amazon's workforce of over 500,000,[9] to take calculated risks in their daily decisions in support of their long-term strategies.[10] The result: A company that's born to disrupt. As Amazon's leaders try out new ideas, the brand's track record of unconventional successes grows longer each year.

This collective appetite for experimentation and risk is one of the reasons behind moonshots such as its Prime subscription delivery service, Kindle e-reader, and $13 billion cloud computing subsidiary, Amazon Web Services.[11] Before these success stories, the idea of an online bookseller delivering food from local restaurants in under an hour (via Amazon Prime), manufacturing its own electronic devices (such as Kindle, Echo, and Dot), or storing data for other major brands such as Airbnb and Netflix (with Amazon Web Services) would have sounded crazy. Today, they're established revenue channels.

Space hotels don't sound so crazy now, do they?

Bezos's commitment to subverting the status quo by taking chances on radical ideas from day 1 is characteristic of the fourth transformation in the modern legacy mindset: from obeying orthodox boundaries to pioneering unconventional solutions.

Transformation:

Nearsighted brand leaders focus on mastering rules (e.g., business is about making profits) and take conventional wisdom for granted (e.g., there are no profits in altruism), all in the interest of maintaining the status quo.

Leaders with the modern legacy mindset forge extraordinary and lasting change by breaking rules, including reconciling paradoxes (e.g., business can make money *and* be a force for good).

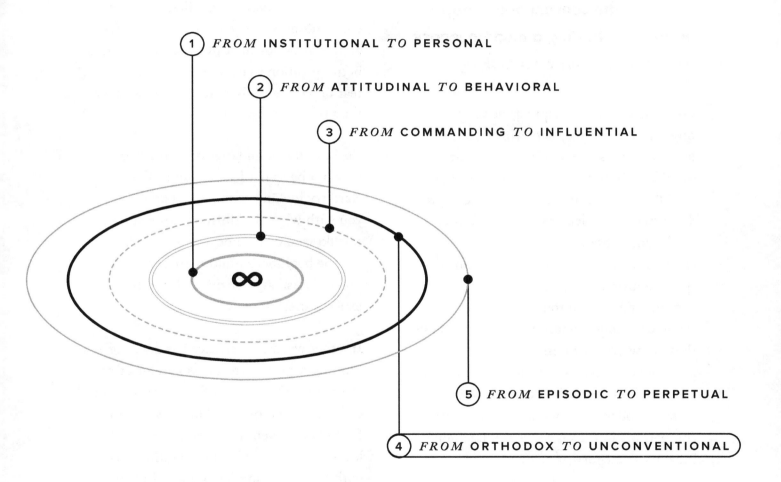

1. *FROM* INSTITUTIONAL *TO* PERSONAL

2. *FROM* ATTITUDINAL *TO* BEHAVIORAL

3. *FROM* COMMANDING *TO* INFLUENTIAL

5. *FROM* EPISODIC *TO* PERPETUAL

4. *FROM* ORTHODOX *TO* UNCONVENTIONAL

Are you simply working to put your brand on the conventional "map," or are you charting a modern legacy on a map of your own making?

Over the last three chapters, we've shown how a modern legacy can evolve from a long-term personal ambition to a shared set of beliefs and behaviors all the way to an influential social movement. In Chapter 4, we speak with leaders at Grey Goose, the Belmont Stakes, and Lexus about channeling their unique, unconventional spirit to invent their own game. To avoid commoditization in today's short-term "now" economy, modern legacy builders like these view every expression of their brand as an opportunity to distinguish themselves and stand out from their competitors. In fact, modern legacy brands don't have competitors in the classic sense. Each one inhabits a category of its own.

Before you begin inventing your own game, however, take a moment to appreciate the existing landscape. Look at the brands that came before yours, including the category rules, why they exist, and who benefits from them. Don't feel the need to master the rules; just become familiar with the conventions. Once you have a contextual appreciation for the category, you'll be in a better position to exploit its vulnerabilities, tear down the walls, and create new space for a brand built to last.

Pushing the boundaries of your category may not be as hard as it sounds. For a start, try looking at the world around you with what Buddhist author Shunryu Suzuki would call a beginner's mind. "In the beginner's mind there are many possibilities," says Suzuki. "But in the expert's there are few."[12]

In other words, experience has a way of limiting experts' perspectives—cluttering them up with all sorts of assumptions, social constructs, and other preconceived notions. Fortunately, even the most experienced leader is still capable of seeing the world with fresh eyes and living like a beginner. Beginners don't see rules; they see problems that need solutions and opportunities to fix what's broken. When we take the time to question conventions and consider unorthodox perspectives—thinking like beginners—we begin to see the world anew.

In many cases, category boundaries are no more than self-imposed limits: imaginary fences fabricated by frustration with a paradox no one else has been willing or able to reconcile. Modern legacy builders such as those in this chapter understand that paradoxes are just puzzles that haven't been solved yet. By resolving the paradoxes, these leaders redefine category boundaries and create entirely new categories of their own.

Because most brands rarely question conventions, choosing instead to operate within the bounds of an established market, standing out can be as straightforward as redrawing the boundaries on your own terms. Take it from Sidney Frank, founder of Grey Goose, and François Thibault, the brand's cellar master; Chris Kay, refounder of the Belmont Stakes and CEO and president of the New York Racing Association; and refounder Mark Templin, recent executive vice president of Lexus International. For these modern legacy builders, being a category of one means leveraging their brands' uniqueness in a world forever tipping toward commodification. By finding ways to fashion something new, often out of something old, each is building a legacy in the making that is like no other.

① # Don't Be the Best— Be the Only One

GREY GOOSE

Established 1997

② ## Define Your Category (Don't Let It Define You)
THE BELMONT STAKES
Established 1867

③ ## Ask Deeper Questions
LEXUS
Established 1989

THE TALE OF Sidney Frank, François Thibault, and the iconic vodka they created is an inspiring story about a modern legacy brand that's unconventional by design. In 1996, neither Frank, an innovative American liquor marketer and distributor, nor Thibault, a gifted French cognac creator and oenologist, was known for vodka expertise, yet they still set out to create the world's first "super-premium" brand. Despite their inexperience, or more likely because of it, the pair managed to launch Grey Goose within a year and guide the brand through years of growth, ultimately allowing the Sidney Frank Importing Company, Inc. to sell it to Bacardi Limited in 2004 for more than $2 billion.[13] Under Bacardi, an independent family-owned company with an unconventional spirit of its own (Bacardi's founders were exiled from Cuba by Fidel Castro in 1960),[14] Grey Goose has continued to disrupt the category by defying convention.

Frank had the vision. Having earned fame and fortune in the 1980s by transforming an unassuming German digestif called Jägermeister into a hip drink sold at American nightclubs, by the 1990s Frank turned his attention to learning more about vodka. After researching the category, he deter-mined that the vast majority of vodka brands were low-quality, tasteless, and largely indistinguishable. Although a handful of better-known imports such as Ketel One, Finlandia, and Absolut stayed above the crowded scrum at the bottom of the category, Frank saw a lot of room for improvement. So much, in fact, that he believed there was an opportunity for a new super-premium brand that would cost two to three times as much as its competitors.

As the quality of the vodka would have to be unique and superb, Frank took his idea to Thibault, a master distiller of one of the world's most sophisticated and refined types of liquor: cognac. A product of the French wine country, Thibault had worked his way from the fields to the position of *maître de chai* ("cellar master") at one of the region's celebrated cognac houses. A hard-earned and highly coveted position, the cellar master is the guardian of quality and style. Each house has only one, and the only way to become one is to be selected from other aspiring apprentices by the retiring master.

The year was 1996, and by that point Frank and Thibault had known each other for

years. A distributor of cognac (not only a refined type of brandy but also one of the most expensive drinks behind the bar), Frank had been coming to Thibault for years with recipe requests for flavored cognacs. The two had developed a friendship, and Thibault, who was young enough to be Frank's son, looked forward to the distributor's unusual requests, such as cognac infused with jasmine flower.

"I love a challenge, and Sidney was always coming up with new ideas," Thibault recalls. "I was motivated to try to surprise him by delivering what he asked for any time he came to me asking for a new recipe."

Frank's last request of Thibault as cellar master at the cognac house was his most unconventional yet. Explaining his market research, Frank asked Thibault to join him in creating the world's first super-premium vodka brand.

Inspired by Frank's confidence and insight, Thibault agreed. The decision would roil France's cognac region, which was a small, tight-knit community unaccustomed to change and steeped in generations of tradi-

tion. Not only was the young cellar master giving up a position many of his colleagues had been working toward their entire careers, he was doing so to make vodka, which was widely regarded as an artless, low-end spirit.

"It was difficult for the region," Thibault remembers. "Everybody in there is really close, and it's difficult for some people to accept that someone is doing something different."

There was just one other detail to work out. "I didn't really have a clue how to actually make vodka," Thibault says. "I didn't know the recipe. I didn't have the ingredients. I didn't even have a recipe book."

"I know you don't," Frank told him. "Because the one I want you to make for me doesn't exist yet."

The clichés about how to succeed in business are innumerable: Climb the ladder, earn your stripes, wait in line, watch and learn. All imply a follow-the-rules and take-your-turn approach to working toward category "best-ness." But this is conventional thinking, and it works only when your aim is conventional success. To skip the line, modern legacy builders don't just aim to do their best, they also ask, "How can I be the only one doing what I do?"

> *"Sidney wanted to create a new category. He wanted to change the course of the whole market."*

This was precisely what Frank and Thibault set out to do when they created Grey Goose. At that time, the vodka market seemed saturated. For hundreds of years,

Grey Goose, produced in France, is the world's first and only super-premium vodka crafted by a cognac cellar master in the *maître de chai* tradition.

Mike Dabell/Getty Images

Cellar master, François Thibault, Grey Goose.

Image courtesy of Grey Goose

almost all vodkas came from the world's "vodka belt," a region that includes countries such as Russia, Poland, and Finland. Although vodka can be made from any starch (generally cereals or potatoes), the regulatory definition of the spirit doesn't leave much room for interpretation. According to the U.S. Bureau of Alcohol, Tobacco, Firearms and Explosives (ATF), "'Vodka' is neutral spirits so distilled, or so treated after distillation with charcoal or other materials, as to be *without distinctive character, aroma, taste, or color.*"[15]

How do you stand out in a category literally defined as odorless, tasteless, colorless, and "without distinctive character"? This is where Frank's vision came into play. To distinguish Grey Goose from its Eastern European competitors, Frank wanted to capitalize on France's reputation for luxury goods. Turning to Thibault, he asked the master distiller to design the first vodka produced in the *maître de chai* tradition, incorporating aroma in the distilling process. The result would be distinctly French in every way, from the ingredients and distillation to the packaging and marketing.

"Sidney wanted to create a new category," Thibault recalls. "He wanted to change the course of the whole market."

Dedicated to making "a great vodka that would last," Thibault spent the next year studying France's climate, soil, and environment to find the best ingredients the country had to offer. Thibault even designed his own distillation process, using a continuous-column copper-filtration still. The final product had a character unlike anything on the market.

"When you create something new, there is nothing to measure yourself against," Thibault says, describing the difference between "bestness" and "onlyness." When you aspire to be the only one doing what you do, he says, "you learn that there is no failure as such, but there is always an opportunity to do better."

While Thibault worked on designing a vodka unlike any other, Frank made sure the branding also would be one of a kind. From the frosted glass to the replaceable corks instead of plastic screw-top caps to swapping out cardboard boxes with wood crates for shipping, every aspect of Grey Goose's branding contributed to the aura of French luxury, and they all blended artfully like the ingredients inside the bottle.

Finally, there was a decision to be made about the price point. When Grey Goose was introduced in 1997, Absolut, the category leader, commanded $15 to $17 a bottle. Frank set the opening price of Grey Goose at around $30. Without accolades, there's no telling how long the brand could have kept charging consumers nearly twice the price of its closest competitor. But soon after Grey Goose debuted, a little-known company called the Beverage Testing Institute named Grey Goose the best-tasting vodka in the world.

Frank took his entire profit for the year—$3 million—and spent it on advertising Grey Goose as "the best-tasting vodka in the world." In a category defined as tasteless, Grey Goose's marketing was going directly against the grain, reconciling a paradox: The better the vodka, the less identifiable its taste.

Other positive reviews followed, and whether it was the taste, the price, or the branding,

Carl Miller/Alamy

consumers couldn't get enough. By the early 2000s, with sales approaching 1.5 million cases, Bacardi came calling.[16]

————————

Though Frank died in 2006, just two years after selling the brand to Bacardi, he spent those years practicing acts of generosity. Even his philanthropy was unconventional. To reward employees for their tenure and to encourage them to stay with Grey Goose after the sale, Frank awarded everyone, from executives to secretaries, a large bonus. Then he donated $100 million to Brown University with the intent that no undergraduate would ever have to drop out—as Frank did at age 18—because he or she was unable to afford tuition.[17] Today, approximately 128 students each year benefit from the scholarship fund in his name.[18]

Thibault elected to keep his day job. Recently celebrating his twentieth anniversary as Grey Goose's cellar master, he continues to bend the category by designing vodkas unlike anything else in the market.

"Grey Goose became number one by taking the lead rather than following the trend," Thibault says. "If something has to be invented, it's Grey Goose that should be doing it."

For Thibault this is not just a trend or short-term tactic—it's a way of life.

"Either you can fall into a routine—something that is always going to be the same—or you have a spirit that likes to discover and experiment," he says.

Frank and Thibault managed to forge a different path: creating a disruptive brand, born to make change, in which the only routine is experimentation. In reconciling this paradox—that is, by making experimentation part of their routine—Grey Goose built a modern legacy that is unconventional by design.

In building your modern legacy, how can you be a category of one?

The brilliance of Frank and Thibault's success with Grey Goose lies in how easy they made it look. Unlike their competitors, who play by category rules, they were able to write their own rules because they aspired to be something different from the start: A category of one.

To ensure that your product or business is not easily replaced, commoditized, or rendered irrelevant, ask yourself how you could authentically become your own category of one. Start by identifying the category conventions. Can you reconcile a paradox and create your own space? Once you've envisioned a category of your own, what practices could you establish that no imitator could easily follow?

Often, as in the next story, being unconventional is less about the conventional competitors you seek to keep out of your category than it is about the unconventional aspects you bring in from the outside world.

Thibault, still pioneering after more than 20 years. Says the brand's cellar master: "Either you can fall into a routine—something that is always going to be the same—or you have a spirit that likes to discover and experiment."

Image courtesy of Grey Goose

1 **Don't Be the Best—Be the Only One**
GREY GOOSE
Established 1997

2 # Define Your Category (Don't Let It Define You)

THE BELMONT STAKES

Established 1867

3 **Ask Deeper Questions**
LEXUS
Established 1989

ON JUNE 7, 2014, California Chrome, an American thoroughbred attempting to become the first horse since 1978 to win horse racing's vaunted Triple Crown of thoroughbred races (consisting of the Kentucky Derby, the Preakness Stakes, and the Belmont Stakes), shot out of the gate alongside 10 other horses at Belmont Park. The morning-line favorite to win, California Chrome stayed close to the front of the pack throughout the race but ultimately crossed the finish line fourth. Witnessed by 21.3 million TV viewers, the anticlimactic finish marked the thirty-sixth consecutive year without a Triple Crown winner and stood as a fitting metaphor for the lackluster state of the sport at large.[19]

"We have lost a generation going back 10, 15, 20 years," admits Chris Kay, CEO and president of the New York Racing Association (NYRA), the organization that runs thoroughbred racing at New York's three major tracks, including the Belmont. "And when we lost that generation, we lost the ability for that generation to bring their kids to the track. They were going to other sporting venues. Football has grown in popularity. Horse racing has declined."

Founded in 1867, Belmont is the oldest of the Triple Crown races. But California Chrome's 2014 loss was a turning point for the venerable organization and for Kay, its newly appointed CEO.

"We had a massive in-person crowd of 102,199," Kay recalls of the 2014 event. "And we didn't have the infrastructure to help make that experience a must-repeat one. The logistics of getting in and out were not good at all."

Overpacked and underwhelmed, the 2014 crowd—the third largest in Belmont history—was bottlenecked by the track's aging Long Island Rail Road (LIRR) train station, which hadn't been updated since 1968. Many attendees spent hours waiting to get home, adding to the anticlimactic atmosphere.

"It was something that I was concerned about and wanted to address as a newcomer," Kay says. "However, I had been told, 'We've been doing this for a long time. This is your first one. Don't worry about it.' The result, as feared, was not good."

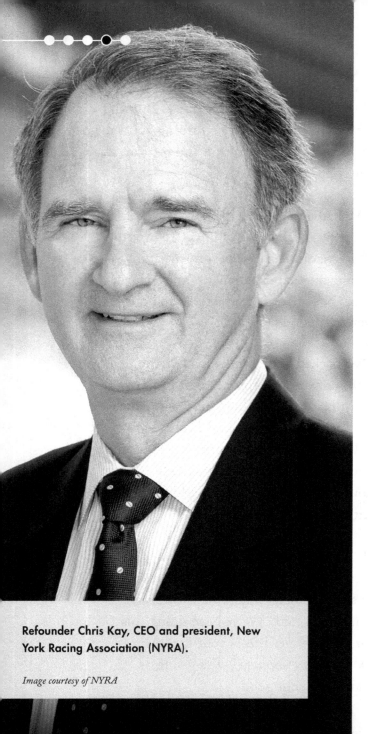

Refounder Chris Kay, CEO and president, New York Racing Association (NYRA).

Image courtesy of NYRA

The Belmont was established to be a must-see event, but what that means has changed a lot since 1867. Reinterpreting the Belmont's iconic status in the contemporary context was Kay's first order of business. After studying the brand's unique attributes during his first year as CEO, he was ready to look beyond horse racing for unconventional ways to reanimate Belmont's legacy in the making.

———————

The conventional approach to "category leadership" is to be better than everyone else in the category. But what happens when your entire category is shrinking? To evolve the brand's modern legacy, Kay is balancing a respect for nearly 150 years of tradition (the Belmont did not run in 1911 and 1912) with an urgent need to reframe horse racing as modern and relevant to younger generations. Rather than benchmarking against its competitors in the field, the Belmont Stakes is benchmarking against what it means to be a must-see event in popular culture, tapping sports fans' evolving tastes in media, technology, and entertainment as a guide.

On the Monday following the 2014 Belmont Stakes, just 36 hours after the crowds had cleared Belmont Park and 363 days before the 2015 race, Kay set in motion a series of changes that were intended to turn the NYRA's marquee brand into a modern must-see event. The initial order of business: infrastructure. The first call Kay made that morning was to the newly appointed president of the LIRR. Working together, the two agreed to spend $5 million to build a new train station capable of serving the Belmont's crowds. A 50-week project, the station would be done just in time for the 2015 event.

Next, Kay announced that he was capping attendance for the 2015 Belmont Stakes at 90,000, which was some 12,000 fewer attendees than in 2014. He knew that even the most loyal fans would quit attending if the in-person experience was that bad every year.

"In response, some people said that I was an idiot and that I was closing out the sport," he says. "But the vast majority of people said, 'I think that shows real courage.'"

Kay was just getting warmed up. To bring the Belmont into the twenty-first century organizers installed nearly 400 high-definition (HD) televisions, three massive HD video boards, an HD slow-motion camera at the finish line, and HD point-of-view cameras that allow fans to customize the way they watch workouts, the paddocks, and the races themselves.

> "The most important thing is to be open to every idea."

"We even tried a drone to give us better shots of the crowd," he says. "But we have not yet utilized a drone to give us shots of the race itself. The balance we need to find is to integrate modern technology to enhance viewing, but not while putting any of the horses or jockeys at risk and not while interfering with the race itself, including how the horses run."

Looking to popular culture for inspiration, organizers at the Belmont Stakes have lined up entertainment such as paratroopers jumping out of helicopters, Broadway stars, and A-list musical acts. Pictured here, the Goo Goo Dolls performing at the 2015 Belmont Stakes.

Image courtesy of NYRA

Beyond capital improvements, ticket sales, and technology, the NYRA's CEO has been transforming the sporting event itself. Until recently, the Belmont was effectively a one-race event in which audience sizes were directly related to whether there was a Triple Crown on the line. For example, if a Triple Crown was up for grabs in recent years, ticket sales pushed 100,000 and millions more watched at home. Without a Triple Crown at stake, track and TV audiences dropped by half.

For perspective, the Triple Crown has been at stake only 35 times during the brand's nearly 150 years (besides 12 wins, there have been 20 unsuccessful bids and three scratches). This means that for nearly a century and a half, revenue at the Belmont Stakes has fluctuated wildly as a result of circumstances entirely out of the brand's control. In essence, like its fans, the NYRA has been gambling with the Belmont Stakes. Kay has set out to change that. To do so, he's willing to look for inspiration outside of horse racing, whether in music, fashion, technology, or wherever else popular culture may lead.

"The most important thing is to be open to every idea," he says. "What I've tried to do is look at all aspects of the business. Because my brand is a sport, I look at other sports and how they've succeeded for inspiration. The same goes for entertainment and casino gaming. Horse racing has not been receptive to too much change. And as we have been catching up with the times, I'm beginning to ask, 'What can we do that no other sport, entertainment, or gaming brand is doing?'"

One way Kay worked to make the Belmont a must-see event was by expanding the event into a three-day festival featuring 31 races, 17 stakes races, and more than $10 million in purse money. Beyond races, organizers have lined up bands and entertainment such as paratroopers with GoPros jumping out of helicopters, Broadway stars, and A-list musical acts. Thematically, Kay is looking beyond horse racing to the culture of nearby New York City for inspiration.

"Beyond tapping into the passion that already exists, our ambition is to turn the Belmont Stakes into even more of a New York tradition. We want to make our event the unofficial start to summer in the same way that the US Open tennis tournament is the unofficial end of summer," he says. "It's

a high ambition, but again, we are building a modern legacy that signals the Belmont as the best day of racing in America."

On June 6, 2015, almost a year to the day after California Chrome's failed Triple Crown bid, millions of viewers were back on the edges of their seats to watch American Pharoah attempt to win the Triple Crown. This time, the crowd got its wish. Winning by five and a half lengths, American Pharoah ended the longest Triple Crown drought in the history of the sport.

For Kay, who spent two years restoring and modernizing every aspect of the Belmont Stakes, horse racing's "crown jewel," it was a transcendent moment.

"The wall of sound that engulfed us on the presentation platform, from about eight seconds before American Pharoah won, up until 10 minutes after, was incredible," he says. "It was so loud and joyous. I turned and looked at all these people on their feet with their arms in the air, everyone jumping up and down."

After looking to culture to breathe new life into the Belmont Stakes, Kay and his colleagues at the NYRA now watched firsthand as the Belmont Stakes returned to the limelight, uniting people all over the world around a few unforgettable moments of shared bliss. While the world watches and waits for another Triple Crown, the Belmont has continued to build its modern legacy by borrowing from culture and reinterpreting it in its own unique way to create a must-see event that is bigger than a horse race.

On June 6, 2015, American Pharoah became the first horse since 1978 to win the Triple Crown, captivating the attention of generations, old and new.

Image courtesy of NYRA

In building your modern legacy, how can you leap over category boundaries?

To weave his brand into the rich cultural fabric of New York, Kay is looking beyond horse racing for broader influences from other must-see events. As a result, what once was just a single, albeit significant, horse race is now transforming into an even larger unconventional cultural event.

To do the same, stop competing conventionally. If you stick to your category lanes, you'll miss new shifts and perspectives in other categories. If all you ever do is look to the immediate left and right for growth, you're going to miss all the change going on elsewhere. Find inspiration in popular culture. See past the category walls with a beginner's mind. What would you incorporate or reapply to distinguish your brand while violating the orthodoxy of your category? How unorthodox could you get without alienating your advocates? If your brand is well established, don't reject the past—enhance your past through a modern lens. Remember: When you throw out the rules and let culture guide you, you can become your only competitor.

Under Chris Kay, the Belmont Stakes' modern legacy continues to evolve in unconventional directions. Says Kay: "What can we do that no other sport, entertainment, or gaming brand is doing?"

Bill Frakes/Getty Images

(1) **Don't Be the Best—Be the Only One**
GREY GOOSE
Established 1997

(2) **Define Your Category (Don't Let It Define You)**
THE BELMONT STAKES
Established 1867

(3) # Ask Deeper Questions

LEXUS

Established 1989

IN AUGUST 1983, Eiji Toyoda, the chairman of Toyota Motor Corporation, called a secret meeting of his best strategists, engineers, designers, and managers.[20] Toyoda had been with the iconic Japanese auto brand from the beginning, helping pioneer its culture of continuous improvement and leading it to profitability. Recently assuming the role of chairman after acting as the brand's longest-serving chief executive, the smartly dressed 69-year-old leader stood before his colleagues, called the secret meeting to order, and calmly delivered the most ambitious challenge in the company's history: He asked them to build the world's best car.

Founded in 1937, Toyota was already known for making efficient, reliable, and affordable vehicles. Americans fell in love with gas-sipping models such as the Corona and the Corolla after the 1973 oil crisis, and by 1978 Toyota had won the "Import Triple Crown," selling more cars, trucks, and total vehicles in the United States than any other import brand. But as baby boomers aged and began buying more luxurious cars, Toyota was losing loyal customers to brands such as Mercedes-Benz and BMW. Mercedes had a three-pointed star. BMW had

a powerful engine. Toyota wanted to offer customers something even better, something more ambitious.

The chairman was asking a lot of his company. For a brand that had built its name on value, the luxury automotive category presented several challenges. To begin with, Toyota's core strengths (efficiency, reliability, and affordability) were not traditional selling points for luxury car buyers. Consumers at the premium end of the automotive market tended to care more about status and scarcity than they did about mileage and maintenance. Moreover, the luxury category was dominated by venerable European marques with longstanding pedigrees and prestige. If Toyota wanted to launch a luxury brand, it would have to overcome the challenge of being new in a category that honored history, tradition, and heritage. In other words, unable to rely on history, the brand had to start making some of its own.

To do that, the brand would have to find a way to change luxury car buyers' appetites. Standing before his top management nearly 35 years ago, Toyota's chairman wasn't just asking the brand to engineer the world's best

vehicle. He was asking it to engineer a profound change in people's hearts and minds. He was asking them to see beyond the now.

"To achieve our highest ambitions, we had to look into the future," explains Mark Templin, recent executive vice president of Lexus International. "If you ask people what they want, they will often tell you something they see in the marketplace today, because consumers don't always know what they want yet."

————————

Presented with a question, the human brain instinctively begins searching for an answer, often before the question is finished. Millennia of hardwired evolution and years of hard-earned experience have honed our minds to seek out quick solutions. Firing instantaneously, intuitively, and unconsciously, our neurons sift through the available data, favoring the familiar and eschewing the unusual. The cognitive result is convention.

Thinking unconventionally, however, requires retraining the brain to invest more effort up front. When you do—when you consider the challenge and decide how to best frame the right question rather than reflexively jumping to a quick resolution—you will begin to think about the problems differently. Moreover, taking the time to ask deeper questions at the outset instead of speeding to the first short-term fix leads to more profound solutions.

Solving problems the unconventional way requires patience, reflection, and curiosity—qualities Toyota was already well known for by 1983. The brand famously thrives on challenges, using them to learn and grow. Taiichi Ohno, pioneer of the Toyota Production System in the 1950s, once stated, "Having no problems is the biggest problem of all."[21] To Ohno, every problem was an opportunity for continuous improvement (*kaizen*) in disguise. He encouraged his staff to "observe the production floor without preconceptions." Then, with every problem, they would ask "why." Once you have your first answer, ask why again. Repeat this cycle five times. For example: Why is the cabin noisy? Because of engine noise. Why is the engine noisy? And so on. After five successively deeper *whys*, you'll not only reach the root causes of your initial problem, you'll probably identify several other problems worth addressing.

> "*We have to look beyond what people want today and ask, 'What will society look like in the future?'*"

To achieve its ambition—to build the world's best luxury car—Toyota would have to question everything about the luxury category, from the way vehicles were manufactured to the way they were marketed. To perform this task, the brand created the F1

Refounder Mark Templin, recent executive vice president of Lexus International.

Image courtesy of Lexus

Toyota Recalls All 8,000 Cars of Lexus Model

Los Angeles Times
December 05, 1989
James Risen | Times Staff Writer

DETROIT — Yes, the Japanese are human too.

Evidence that they sometimes make mistakes came Monday, when Toyota announced a voluntary recall of all 8,000 of the Lexus LS 400 luxury cars it has sold since the Lexus line was introduced in September.

Officials at Toyota's Lexus division said Monday that they had notified the federal government Friday that Toyota is issuing a recall on the cars to make three repairs.

Lexus' first recall comes at an awkward moment for Toyota—right in the midst of the auto maker's highly publicized launch of the new luxury car line. Toyota has been promoting Lexus as a car that is as good as a BMW or a Mercedes-Benz—but which costs much less—and has built its advertising around the slogan that Lexus is the product of a "relentless pursuit of perfection."

. . .

"We've always said that customer satisfaction is our first priority, and this is an opportunity to prove that," Lexus spokesman Kurt Von Zumwalt said.[22]

Excerpts from a *Los Angeles Times* article reporting on Lexus's 1989 recall—one of the brand's earliest defining moments.

Permission via the Los Angeles Times

Project (short for Flagship One), staffing it with thousands of researchers, engineers, technicians, and designers. In time, the F1 Project would become known as a new brand: Lexus.[23] But first, before the team began designing the car or researching the competition, it wanted to understand the customer.

"Many brands inside and outside of our industry always talk about their product— it's all about the product," says Templin, who during his long tenure with Toyota is credited for being among the leaders who helped guide the development of the Lexus brand. "Well, why does the product exist in the first place? It exists for the consumer."

Although any brand can ask customers what they want, the Lexus team sought out the right problem—not "what do customers want?" but "what *will* customers want?"

"We have to look beyond what people want today and ask, 'What will society look like in the future?'" Templin explains. "It's not what people want now but what will they want tomorrow? This thinking allows us to prepare for that future and exceed their expectations."

By focusing on luxury consumers and seeking to anticipate their desires, Lexus researchers arrived at a smarter solution to the chairman's initial challenge. To change hearts and minds in the luxury category, the Lexus team would do more than build the world's best car. It would offer the world's best care and the world's best experience, beginning at the dealership and continuing long after the customer purchased a vehicle. This insight culminated in the brand's enduring covenant.

"The covenant made three key points that created strong foundations for the brand," Templin recalls. "It said we would have the finest dealer network in the industry, that we would make the finest cars ever built, and that we would treat each customer as we would a guest in our home."

Between 1983 and 1989, the Lexus team devoted all of its resources—70 designers, 24 teams (made up of 1,400 engineers, 2,300 technicians, and 220 support workers), approximately 450 prototypes, and hundreds of millions of dollars in costs—to ensure that the new luxury brand lived up to the three key points in its ambitious cov-

enant.[24] As it turned out, their efforts would be put to the test just three months after the brand's launch.

———————

Launched in September 1989, the Lexus brand was an instant success. Consumers called Lexus's flagship model, the LS 400, the best car they'd ever bought. *Car and Driver* named it one of the 10 Best Cars of the year. The brand's 81 dealerships sold 2,919 LS 400s in the first month alone, averaging more than one a day, or about nine a week per dealership.

By December, however, the fledgling brand found itself mired in a crisis and facing a critical decision point. With 8,000 LS 400s already on the road, customers had identified three product defects: a sticky cruise control function, warping plastic around the high-mounted rear brake light, and a faulty connection that could drain the battery. Although no accidents or injuries had been reported and the National Highway Traffic Safety Administration was not even aware

> *"We want to keep changing the industry for the better. We want to always act like the challenger brand that is trying to do something new and think into the future."*

"Everyone looked at the covenant and said, 'How would you treat a customer as a guest in your home?'" Templin recalls. "If they had this issue, would you fix it or would you brush it off?"

When your rallying cry is "the relentless pursuit of perfection," brushing it off isn't an option. Putting its customers' well-being first, Lexus issued the recall. Where other brands might have mailed out a recall notice on a postcard, Lexus called each of its 8,000 LS customers personally.

If customers wanted to come in to the dealership, Lexus welcomed them. If not, Lexus came to them. "We put technicians on airplanes to fly three hours to remote locations to fix cars at customers' homes," says Templin. "We left customers with Lexus service loaners so they wouldn't be inconvenienced during the period of time we were fixing their car. We gave them their car back with a full tank of gas and apologized for the inconvenience. Ultimately, it showed people what we stood for, what our culture was and what we wanted to be."

of the defects, Lexus made the decision to recall its flagship voluntarily. Once again, rather than basing this decision on the impact it would have on the brand's short-term reputation or finances, Lexus looked to its customers to understand the problem from their perspective.

Luxury car buyers noticed.

Lexus customers became the brand's best marketers, changing hearts and minds much faster than anyone had predicted. By 1991, Lexus (then just two years old) became the bestselling luxury import in the United States, outselling Mercedes-Benz (established in 1926) and BMW (established in 1916). By 2000, Lexus was only 11 years old and the brand had surpassed Lincoln (established in 1917) and Cadillac (established in 1902) to become the nation's top-selling luxury brand overall. Globally, 2016 was Lexus International's fourth consecutive record sales year. Though Eiji Toyoda died in 2013, the luxury brand he inspired continues to set sales records in markets around the world.

In the nearly three decades since its launch, Lexus has never stopped asking deeper questions in the spirit of innovating and building a better luxury car. The brand has had many "world's firsts" since 1989, including being the first to win J.D. Power's "triple crown" (sales satisfaction, initial quality, and customer satisfaction), the first to build a car-based luxury SUV (the RX), and the first luxury brand to build both a hybrid SUV (the RXh) and a high-performance hybrid (the GSh). Templin attributes these and thousands of other innovations to the brand's unwavering belief in better understanding its customers. As Lexus engineers are fond of saying, "The more we know about the driver, the more we know about the automobile." This belief, Templin claims, has broader indirect benefits for everyone, not just Lexus and its customers.

"We want to keep changing the industry for the better," Templin says. "We want to always act like the challenger brand that is trying to do something new and think into the future."

Recently, Lexus engineers began working with urban planners in cities around the world to design safer streets. A luxury automotive brand helping rewrite the rules of the road from the ground up? Yes, it's unconventional. But that's how the brand has always behaved—seeking tomorrow's problems in the name of reaching unique solutions.

In building your own modern legacy, how can you tell your own fortune?

In a short-term world, telling employees what to do is a form of efficiency. From this perspective, questions slow everyone down. In contrast, because they think unconventionally, modern legacy builders understand that when leaders stop asking deeper questions, their brands get stuck in the past. Instead of wasting their time running in circles and chasing short-term goals with short-term solutions, modern legacy builders encourage their employees to focus on the future to bring the past forward.

By seeking out the right problems, such as what drivers will want years from now, not just today, Lexus always has a consistent pipeline of unconventional ideas to drive its legacy in the making into the future.

What questions can you ask about the long-term future of your modern legacy that might shed some light on the near term? What problems need solving? The more insightful your questions are, the more insightful your answers will be. Try using your "beginner's mind" to ask questions that reach beyond conventions. Then ask *why* five times without settling for the first four answers. Not only will you derive more insight from these methods, you'll get more foresight. The best way to see into the future is to write it yourself.

The 2013 Lexus LFA, a $375,000 supercar. The design of the LFA is so advanced, Lexus engineers had to pioneer multiple new manufacturing methods, including the creation of a carbon fiber loom (later celebrated in London's Design Museum). There are only 500 LFAs in existence.

Image courtesy of Lexus

 **Summation**

Although each of the stories in this chapter illustrates a different way in which modern legacy brands are born unconventional, it's notable that all these brands draw insight and identity from the very rules they break. In this way, they live like beginners, questioning and reshaping the status quo. In turn, they stand out for significant and meaningful innovations. It makes sense, after all. What is an iconoclast without conventions to clash with?

For Grey Goose, the rules of the category were clear: Vodka came from Eastern Europe. It was cheap, flavorless, and pretty much all the same. Though Sidney Frank and François Thibault could have set out to create the best brand in the established market, that would have meant playing by the existing category rules. Instead, they positioned themselves in a category of their own as the world's first super-premium vodka, an artisanal French brand in a tasteless, odorless segment of the liquor market. To reinforce their identity and make it durable, they reconciled a paradox as "the world's best-tasting vodka." The lesson: When you do something that no one else is doing, you set your own standard.

As Thibault says, there's nothing to measure yourself against. In turn, you become the measure for yourself and others.

Breaking convention by looking outside its category, the Belmont Stakes is co-opting innovations from other leading forms of entertainment, such as professional football and music festivals, and reapplying them in the unique context of horse racing in order to stand out. After losing a generation of fans, Chris Kay understood that not all the old rules of horse racing were working and nearly a century and a half of tradition needed refreshing. By tapping trends outside the category, Kay incorporated new ideas and leveraged culture to guide the brand into the modern age—and continues to do so.

Finally, up against venerable titans such as Mercedes and BMW, Lexus could have played by the category rules and focused solely on building the best product. Instead, as Mark Templin shared, the brand asked questions, such as, "Why does the product exist in the first place?" and "What will the customer want tomorrow?" Because it continues to ask deeper questions, Lexus is able to stay out in front of category conventions decades after it was established. In a category traditionally defined by old-world luxury, the brand challenged the rules and focused on how to serve modern consumers and society better. As a result, Lexus has been able to reshape the entire luxury automotive market.

No one forges extraordinary and lasting change by playing by the established rules or protecting the status quo. This is not to say that the key to being unconventional is simply being different. Grey Goose, the Belmont Stakes, and Lexus were founded by and continue to be led by rare leaders who are fully aware of the conventions of their categories even as their brands evolve. From there, they can invent their own game by becoming categories of one, letting popular culture inspire them, and asking deeper questions. As their continued success proves, copies tend to fade, but originals endure.

| THE LEGACY BUILDER'S BALANCE SHEET | *The Weight of Worth* |

It's a classic juxtaposition in the world of marketing: On one end are brands with high value (attractive at a low price), and on the other end are brands with high worth (worth it at almost any price). In recent years, the landmark TCL Chinese Theatre on the historic Hollywood Walk of Fame found itself at risk of tipping toward the wrong end of The Legacy Lab's Worth-Value Scale.

Founded by Sid Grauman in 1927, the iconic Chinese Theatre has long been "the place" for major Hollywood film premieres and a mecca for devotees of the film industry. Generations of film lovers have flocked there just to attend a show—any show—in the legendary venue. During the last decade, however, the rise of better home theater systems and video capabilities on phones and tablets has forced theaters everywhere to improve the movie-watching experience and rethink how they appeal to the viewing public, altering the worth-value dynamic for the entire film industry. The shift has even had an impact at a one-of-a-kind venue like the Chinese Theatre, which still premieres more major films than any other theater on Earth. In the face of these challenges, refounder Alwyn Hight Kushner, the brand's president and chief operating officer, recently initiated several changes to reinforce the Theatre's storied legacy in the making.

"We can't have Steven Spielberg watching his own movie and have it not be perfect," says Hight Kushner. "When you have the most esteemed filmmakers of our time coming to watch and experience their movies, our presentation has to be remarkable."

To ensure that the Theatre keeps its unique worth and status in the eyes of filmmakers and audiences alike, the brand underwent a massive, months-long renovation, adding all the latest

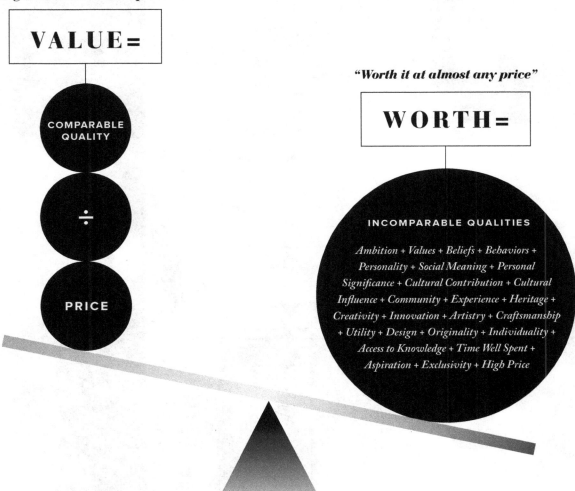

"A good value at a low price"

VALUE =

COMPARABLE QUALITY

÷

PRICE

"Worth it at almost any price"

WORTH =

INCOMPARABLE QUALITIES

Ambition + Values + Beliefs + Behaviors + Personality + Social Meaning + Personal Significance + Cultural Contribution + Cultural Influence + Community + Experience + Heritage + Creativity + Innovation + Artistry + Craftsmanship + Utility + Design + Originality + Individuality + Access to Knowledge + Time Well Spent + Aspiration + Exclusivity + High Price

Weigh In

Brands that are easy to compare and brands that are beyond compare fall at opposite ends of The Legacy Lab's Worth-Value Scale. The TCL Chinese Theatre invests in unique qualities that distinguish it from other theaters to boost its worth among consumers. What are you doing to fill your brand with worth? Avoid tipping towards conventional value by investing in those intangible qualities—such as your contributions to culture and community—that make your brand incomparable and irreplaceable.

Source: The Legacy Lab

From left, founder Sid Grauman with actress Gloria Swanson, the Theatre's iconic exterior, and refounder Alwyn Hight Kushner, the brand's president and chief operating officer.

Images courtesy of TCL Chinese Theatres

cutting-edge technology and creature comforts while meticulously retaining the Theatre's singular atmosphere and experience. As a result, the Theatre now claims one of the largest IMAX screens in the world and the largest IMAX auditorium. Annually, more than 5 million people visit the fabled Theatre, including the many celebrities attending red-carpet premieres. Each blockbuster crowd spilling out onto Hollywood Boulevard—just steps from the handprints and footprints of nearly a century of Hollywood stars in the Theatre's courtyard—provides further evidence that the brand's unique modern legacy is worth the trip.

Although value brands are easy to compare, worth brands—such as the Chinese Theatre—are beyond compare. Imagine your brand on the Worth-Value Scale on page 169. On which end does it fall? To add worth, consider what factors would further distinguish your brand. Can you claim rare qualities such as artistry, craft, and exclusivity? How else could you invest in fewer, more distinctive expressions to ensure that your modern legacy is beyond compare?

CHAPTER FIVE

Never Stop Making Legacy

"There's an inherent danger in letting people think that they have perfected something. When they believe they've 'nailed it,' most people tend to sit back and rest on their laurels while countless others will be laboring furiously to better their work!"

SIR RICHARD BRANSON

Founder of the Virgin Group[1]

THE VIRGIN GROUP, a conglomerate with more than 60 businesses around the world,[2] got its start as a mail-order record company back in 1970, when its founder, Richard Branson, was just 19 years old.[3] As he and his colleagues were new to the music business, Branson chose the name Virgin. The decision—like many during his career—was appropriate, irreverent, and prescient.

Despite never attending college or business school, Branson subsequently led Virgin into a multitude of disparate industries over a half century, from banking, travel, and entertainment to health and fitness, transportation, communications, and more.[4] Never content to sit still, the tireless entrepreneur has waged a career-long battle against complacency and the status quo, advising fellow entrepreneurs to know their objectives, pay attention to detail, and continually improve.[5] Because of Branson's vigilant leadership and focus, all Virgin businesses share the brand's core DNA: mischief, imagination, and tireless diligence.

True to form, Branson exhibits the same trademark boldness and tenacity in his personal pursuits as he does in his professional life. He is a world-record holder in kite surfing, hot-air ballooning,[6] and high-speed boating,[7] and even his failed attempts at world records speak to his perseverance, bringing him one step closer to eventual success. Now worth an estimated $5 billion,[8] Branson says organizations can draw inspiration from the diligence it takes to set world records.

"Guinness World Records are tangible proof that humans can achieve incredible things if we work together and set our mind to it," he writes on Virgin's website. "Nobody breaks records—or builds successful businesses—without being dedicated."[9]

For continually striving to improve in every aspect of his life and work, Branson embodies the fifth transformation necessary to build a modern legacy: from episodic innovation to perpetual adaptation.

Transformation:

Nearsighted brand leaders tend
to grow stale by repeating the past
or to lose their identity
by renouncing it.

**Leaders with the modern legacy
mindset find a new way, cultivating
enduring significance by bringing the
past forward and reinvigorating their
brands each day.**

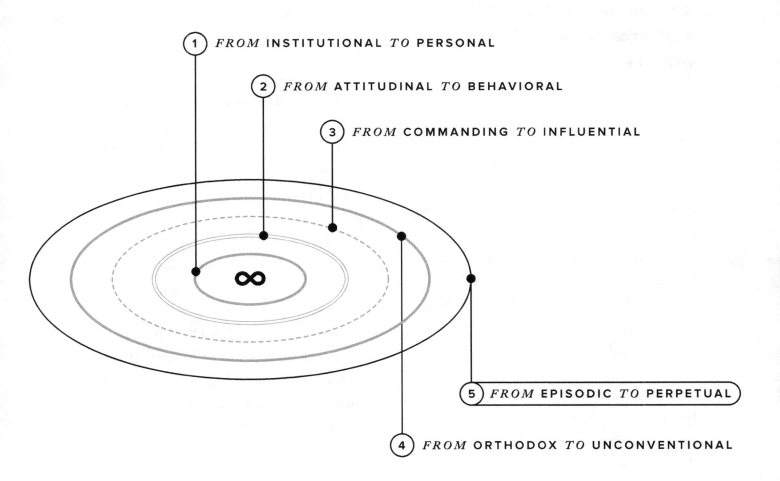

1 *FROM* INSTITUTIONAL *TO* PERSONAL

2 *FROM* ATTITUDINAL *TO* BEHAVIORAL

3 *FROM* COMMANDING *TO* INFLUENTIAL

5 *FROM* EPISODIC *TO* PERPETUAL

4 *FROM* ORTHODOX *TO* UNCONVENTIONAL

Are your daily efforts just a means to a short-term end, or are they a reflection of your ambition without end?

Over the last four chapters, we've shown how modern legacy builders bring their brands to life. In Chapter 5, we explore how they keep them that way—alive and thriving for years to come. As modern legacy building never ends, we've devoted this last chapter to illustrating how enduring brands such as the Toronto Maple Leafs, The Championships, Wimbledon, and Taylor Guitars are making legacy every day.

We've all heard some variation of the truism about the dynamic nature of life and work: If you're not evolving, you're dying. If you're not growing, you're dying. If you're not learning . . . well, you get the idea. Regardless of the verb, the alternative to dynamism is death. Modern legacies

are no different. If you're not perpetually adding to your legacy in the making, it's neither modern nor in the making. At that point, it's just a traditional legacy.

Brands that cease to evolve inevitably die in today's short-term economy. Some fade away, calling out from the past like old songs stuck on repeat. Others sputter, evolving in fits and starts, out of sync with the times. Sooner or later, however, they all suffer the same fate. Although we could fill this book with cautionary tales of iconic brands that lost their relevance, all those stories have the same moral: Once you stop making history, you become a part of it.

To stay vigilant and keep their brands vital, each of the modern legacy builders in this chapter is finding unique ways to incorporate long-term personal ambitions into everyday practices and habits. At the Toronto Maple Leafs, refounder Brendan Shanahan, the president and alternate governor, doesn't just have a plan for building a championship hockey team, he's showing others how to stick with it year after year, through the highs and lows. At The Championships, Wimbledon, refounder and CEO of the All England Lawn Tennis Club (AELTC) Richard Lewis is letting the brand's storied past inform the present. At Taylor Guitars, cofounders Kurt Listug and Bob Taylor are passing their legacy in the making forward to ensure that their passion transcends generations. Informed by the past and drawn by the future, each of these leaders is applying discipline and focus to forge a modern legacy perpetually—today, tomorrow, and always.

① Don't Just Have a Plan, Stick with It

THE TORONTO MAPLE LEAFS

Established 1917

② Let the Past Inform the Present
THE CHAMPIONSHIPS, WIMBLEDON
Established 1877

③ Transcend Generations
TAYLOR GUITARS
Established 1974

GROWING UP just outside Toronto, Canada, Brendan Shanahan spent a lot of Saturday nights watching the Toronto Maple Leafs play on *Hockey Night in Canada*.

"The team won 13 Stanley Cups going back to 1918," says the former National Hockey League (NHL) star. "But when I grew up, the team was not great."

The Leafs won their last championship in 1967, meaning that Shanahan, who was born in 1969, went to bed hanging his head many Saturday nights. For several years during his youth, the team didn't even make the playoffs. Flash forward to the present day, and not much has changed. The Leafs' drought between championships—50 years as of 2017—is the longest in the NHL. But Shanahan is working to change all that.

Shanahan got the call to come home to Toronto and take over the Leafs in 2014, after the team missed the playoffs for the ninth time in the previous 10 years. An Olympic gold medalist with Team Canada, high-profile executive with the NHL, and 2013 inductee into hockey's Hall of Fame, Shanahan brought grand ambitions with him.

"I wanted to come back to my hometown and do my best to restore the team to its origins," he says. "The Toronto Maple Leafs should be the New York Yankees of hockey."

Hired as the team's president and alternate governor, Shanahan spent his first year observing the players, coaches, and management.

"Our goal is to build an era of championship hockey in Toronto," he explains. "I was purposefully quiet with the media in my first year. I had a vision in my head, and I wanted to learn for myself in that first season which people in the organization wanted to be a part of it."

The season ended on a Saturday. On Sunday, Shanahan fired roughly 26 people, including the head coach, various assistant coaches, 18 team scouts, and other key personnel. On Monday, he held a press conference. His message was clear: "We're gonna build the front office, we're gonna recruit young talent. And the team is gonna suck at first. Brace yourself for years of pain. But someday, years from now, we're gonna start winning."

Refounder Brendan Shanahan, president and alternate governor, the Toronto Maple Leafs.

Jonathan Bielaski/Getty Images

"It was my first time ever having a press conference like that," he recalls, "and I got some good advice: Be brutally honest. That advice actually transcends addressing the press. Whether it is with owners, players, or staff, be clear and honest about your vision. People don't like surprises, and they don't like being misled."

The media came to call it the Shanaplan.

Championship teams aren't built in one season. They take years of planning, cooperation, and diligence. Shanahan could have stanched the bleeding by keeping veterans or paying to bring in proven stars. The team might have qualified for the playoffs the next year. But that was short-term thinking, and the Leafs' leaders had been trying that for years. Shanahan's ambition was to build a perennial contender for the Stanley Cup.

"It was freeing for me to say that this is what we are, this is what we're not, this is what we want to be, and this is what we're going to try to do," he recalls of that initial press conference after the firings. "And we're not going to stop until we get there."

As he surveyed the room—with the media in front of him, the team on his back, and fans everywhere watching—one question lingered in his mind:

"Who has the stomach to stick with it?"

———————

Building a championship hockey team, like any legacy in the making, is easier said than done. There are those who believe that coming up with the big idea or the master plan is the hard part—the light bulb illuminates, the genius plan takes shape on the back of a napkin in a moment of feverish inspiration, and the rest is just details. If only that were so. Realizing long-term ambitions means sticking with the plan through good times and bad. The Toronto Maple Leafs are trying to do just that.

Of course, Shanahan wasn't the first person to show up in Toronto with big plans for the hometown team. In the 11 years before his arrival, the Leafs had two different ownership groups and five different head coaches.

During that stretch, the team made the playoffs only once.

It's been a familiar pattern since 1967. New owners, new coaches, and new players provided loyal Leafs fans with brief glimpses of brilliance, for example, when the team finished the regular season high in the rankings in 1993–1994 and 2003–2004. But moments of optimism were regularly followed by heartbreak in the playoffs, false-hope draft picks, ill-advised trades, bitter firings, or prolonged rough stretches in which the team failed to make the postseason.

"There is a generation that has mostly known the Toronto Maple Leafs to be one of hockey's punch lines," says Shanahan. "They might remember the trades that gave the team a little spark, a couple of mostly short playoff runs, and a tiny window of hope. But now we have to keep our ongoing ambition in perspective. This is about finishing and not just having a two- or three-year window. We want a championship era."

Shanahan understands what it takes to build a winning team starting from the inside out. One of the top 100 players in NHL history, he was a star with the Detroit Red Wings from 1996 to 2006, helping the Red Wings bring home the Stanley Cup in 1997, 1998, and 2002.

> ## "Today's Leafs are not just playing for themselves. They are playing for the ongoing legacy of the team."

To press reset on the Leafs, Shanahan traded its biggest star—Phil Kessel, a leader some thought was unlikely to buy into the new system—for a first-round draft pick and prospect nine years younger. Two years later, the *Toronto Sun* would call it an "influential and historical trade that has turned out to be enormous. . . . The Leafs have been demonstrating the benefits, tangibly and otherwise, from the Kessel deal all season long—and some will tell you, last season as well."

To rebuild the team, the Leafs hired head coach Mike Babcock. Babcock is the first and only hockey coach to join the esteemed "Triple Gold Club," having guided the Red Wings to a Stanley Cup in 2008 and led Team Canada to a world championship in 2004 and an Olympic gold medal in both 2010 and 2014.

For the general manager position—the executive responsible for overseeing everything from negotiating players' contracts and selecting draft picks to the administration of the team office—the Leafs hired Lou Lamoriello, the only current general manager in the Hockey Hall of Fame, recognized as one of the sport's great architects of championship-winning teams.

"There are certain people that, like certain mountain climbers, will always choose to climb the easiest hills in order to make progress," says Shanahan. "And there are those who instead will always choose to climb the hardest hills, the highest mountains, in order to go further. Our team leaders are all the second type: It is programmed into their DNA to climb higher in order to go further. None of us have to be here. We all want to be here."

With the Leafs' key leadership in place, the front office turned its attention to the team itself. Rather than adding players to improve, the Leafs subtracted, freeing up space for promising new draft picks and talented prospects rising from the farm system. The process continues, says Shanahan, and it's going to take a lot of time and effort—a familiar mantra at the core of the Shanaplan.

"The perception of the Toronto Maple Leafs when I arrived was that the team wasn't stocked with enough good talent," he says. "In my eyes, the big issue wasn't that the team had a talent issue so much as it had a work ethic issue. The team did not always work hard, they crumbled under pressure, they did not demonstrate grit, and they were not so willing to sacrifice as a group. They didn't behave like a team. That reality, in this city where hockey is revered, is unforgivable."

The Maple Leafs' long-term ambition to build a durable, continually successful team with young players—maximizing opportunity in the future—is in stark contrast to those who minimize risk in the near term by spending more today in hopes of buying a better team as quickly as possible.

As if the goal of building a championship team weren't hard enough, the last step—changing the culture of an organization after a half century of losing—may pose the most difficult challenge yet to the Leafs' plan of creating the next NHL dynasty.

———————

Fortunately for the Leafs, the team's past—winning 13 championships between 1918 and 1967—is playing a helpful role in writing its future. Shanahan decided he needed to bring the tradition of winning forward into the modern era and to make it part of a perpetually successful mindset. One way of doing this was creating Legends Row. This 30-foot granite bench is situated just outside the arena in Maple Leaf Square and features

bronzed statues of the team's greatest players. Legends Row reminds fans and players alike of the team's championship heritage. Since its creation in 2014, 14 statues have been added.

"What I feel makes Legends Row particularly noteworthy is that we do focus on a team of honorees from across generations," Shanahan says. "No great player ever stands by himself in Legends Row because he never stood by himself on the ice. He was always surrounded by teammates. Further, it allows us to signal to our current players that they are, today, at the very beginning of giving themselves an opportunity to be added to Legends Row in the future. And it allows us to bring a new generation of fans back to the enduring story of the Toronto Maple Leafs too. Today's Leafs are not just playing for themselves. They are playing for the ongoing legacy of the team."

Just as Conn Smythe, the legendary team owner from 1927 to 1961, evolved the team's former name, the Toronto St. Patricks, and adopted the maple leaf as the team's name and logo to build a better connection with local fans, Shanahan has revitalized the team's iconography. Under his leadership, the team

has updated its uniforms, including the crest: a more detailed maple leaf featuring a vein for each Stanley Cup the team has won. Shanahan even petitioned the league to allow a bigger leaf on the front of the uniform.

"There are lot of little details like these that we thought of," he says. "We fought hard for that. We want the crest to be this big badge that we wear proudly on our chests."

Although playing championship hockey is ultimately the most important way back to a Stanley Cup, Shanahan stresses that restoring aspects of the team's winning identity and culture is an important part of that plan.

Ultimately, every move Shanahan makes—from the players on the team to the uniforms they wear—is intended to put the team in the best position to win.

"When I was a player, before a game, people would often say, 'Good luck tonight. Score a goal,'" he recalls. "In return I would say, 'I'll try.'"

Some people would confuse his response for a lack of confidence. Why not say, "I will"?

Because no player, no matter how good, can make himself score.

"What you can make yourself do is practice your shot, practice the quickness of your release, practice going to all of the right spots, and work to have the fitness to get to the right spot at the right time so you can get four, five, or six shots on goal," Shanahan explains. "This is the same approach to how we are trying to win a Cup. We want to build an organization that gives itself the highest probability to win year after year."

Since Shanahan took over, the Leafs are doing just that. Though the team finished last in the league in 2015–2016, it made the playoffs the very next season, only the second time in 12 years. Though they lost in the first round to the Washington Capitals, their youth and tenacity carried them through six tough games (five of which were decided by one goal in overtime), farther than anyone expected. Looking ahead, the team, the organization, and the fans are more optimistic than they have been in years. With a plan for the Leafs' legacy in the making in place, and a leader intending to make sure everyone in the organization sticks with it perpetually, they have reason to be.

An icon on Legends Row. "[This] allows us to signal to our current players that they are, today, at the very beginning of giving themselves an opportunity to be added to Legends Row in the future."

Tara Walton/Getty Images

In building your modern legacy, how could you practice your plan and perfect your practice?

The number of Shanaplan lessons for rebuilding the Toronto Maple Leafs into a championship team would cram the back of a napkin:

- Be clear and honest about your vision.
- Be self-assured through good times and bad.
- Make sure everyone is on board.
- Hire the very best.
- Strip away complexity.
- Put the team before the star.
- Invest in the future.
- Respect the past.
- Lead with pride.

The list could go on and on.

Collectively, these discrete lessons manifest Shanahan's master plan: Do everything possible to put the team in a position to succeed and then stick with it. Without these daily practices, the master plan is just a dream.

Although there is no such thing as a guarantee of success, like Shanahan, you can practice to win. To do that, incorporate your long-term personal ambitions into everyday practices and habits. Practicing those everyday lessons perpetually is the secret to building your legacy in the making one day at a time.

Does your legacy in the making have a master plan for achieving success like that of the Maple Leafs? What daily practices make it possible? If your plan seems foolproof, ask yourself if you've aimed high enough. Although short-term thinkers seldom tolerate risk, looking for fail-safe shortcuts, long-term thinkers take chances and make sacrifices, sticking to an ambitious plan to perpetually put themselves in a position to succeed.

A new mural, installed by Shanahan in 2017, stands just outside the Leafs' locker room. Emblazoned with "HONOUR, PRIDE, COURAGE" — words originally introduced to the team's crest by legendary owner, general manager, and coach Conn Smythe in 1927 — the mural also includes the names of every player who helped win the team's 13 championships.

Mark Blinch/Getty Images

1 Don't Just Have a Plan, Stick with It
THE TORONTO MAPLE LEAFS
Established 1917

2 # Let the Past Inform the Present

THE CHAMPIONSHIPS, WIMBLEDON

Established 1877

3 Transcend Generations
TAYLOR GUITARS
Established 1974

THE CHAMPIONSHIPS, Wimbledon is the world's most enduring and most esteemed tennis tournament and the only one of the four Grand Slam tournaments played on grass. Although steeped in tradition, however, Wimbledon is no stranger to change. In 2009, for example, after hosting tournament play under the open sky since 1877, the organization did something unprecedented in its history by unveiling a massive high-tech multimillion-dollar retractable roof over the hallowed Centre Court.

Although reactions to the roof were generally positive, not everyone loved the dramatic break from tradition. Britain's number-one player at the time, Andy Murray, claimed the roof's shadow interfered with play, and spectators wondered why only certain seats were afforded its shade when the roof was partially closed on hot days. Then there were the staunch traditionalists who mourned the end of an era. The *New York Times* reported at the time, "[T]here are those who feel that the roof robs Wimbledon of its ineffable spirit, the spirit that believes in triumphing over adversity and making do with unfortunate events."[10] As with most things Wimbledon, everyone had an opinion. "We could have said well, we are an outdoor event, therefore, we won't have a roof," says Richard Lewis, CEO of the AELTC and Wimbledon. "We could have stayed with a narrow viewpoint. But we made a meaningful change for the betterment of the play."

The addition of a modern retractable roof at Wimbledon is a fitting metaphor for the way the esteemed institution nimbly interprets its ambition. Since 1877, the notorious British rainy season has at times interrupted tournament play, left players sidelined for hours, disappointed fans, and, more recently, created headaches for TV networks attempting to broadcast the matches on a schedule. Rather than continue adhering to tradition for tradition's sake, Wimbledon made the decision to draw on an even deeper aspect of its history and identity in choosing to modernize with a retractable roof—the organization's devotion to providing the world's best tennis.

"[The roof] changes the nature of the tournament," Lewis acknowledges. "But it's the right thing to do if it's a change for the better. We must continue to embrace technology where appropriate and not be hamstrung by tradition and history where it's inappropriate."

Though the tournament itself only lasts a couple weeks each summer,[11] living up to Wimbledon's ambition to be "the pinnacle of the sport" is a year-round task. Because all decisions, no matter how minor, must align with the brand's traditions and aspirations, employees add any new concern to "The List"—an evolving set of priorities requiring attention ahead of next year's tournament.

"The list is something that begins during the championships," says Lewis. "The list of all the things we can do better. It goes right to the heart of not accepting second best. We don't really mind where we get the feedback from. If it's something that can't be dealt with immediately, then it goes on the list. Every single line on the list has to have a comment by it by next year's championships. The moment you are satisfied and think that you can't improve on it, that's the moment you've got a problem. We just want it to be better every day and every year."

☐ Tidy foliage

☐ Review signage

☐ Align benches

☐ Control temperature

☐ Review tea blends

☐ Match petunia shades

☐ Repair chipped railing

☐ Fix squeaky chairs

☐ Ease crowd congestion

Indeed, at Wimbledon, any change—such as discontinuing the longstanding requirement that players bow to British royalty before each match—is vetted extensively against the brand's enduring vision. Customs have come and gone over the decades, but Wimbledon's modern legacy of representing the pinnacle of the sport remains perpetual.

Short-term thinkers traditionally have been limited to two perspectives when it comes to traditional legacy: Protect history at all costs or cut it loose to move on. Eschewing both perspectives, modern legacy builders let the past inform the present. At Wimbledon, modern legacy becomes perpetual through equal parts ambition and adaptation.

"There is ongoing internal pressure to question and check that what we did last year is what we should do in the coming year," says Lewis. "The internal pressure to review, challenge, question, and check is all motivated by a shared love for the game of tennis."

Simultaneously serving as guardian of the past and ambassador of the future, Wimbledon has adopted some profound changes over the years. All were made in the interest of better tennis. For example, in 1922, after decades at the original location, the tournament was moved. The new and bigger grounds allowed more people to attend, while the new Centre Court's octagonal shape remains iconic to this day.

Nearly half a century later, in 1968, Wimbledon embraced another fundamental change when it helped usher in "the open era," inviting professional players, not just amateurs, to participate. More recently, the longstanding tradition of requiring players to bow to members of the British Royal Family as they came onto Centre Court was discontinued at the request of the club's president, the Duke of Kent. The only remaining exceptions are for the Queen and the Prince of Wales. Lewis emphasizes that every tradition, and every change to tradition, is meaningful.

"We value continuity and tradition here at Wimbledon," Lewis emphasizes. "We don't make change, physical or cultural, without

serious consideration. It's never change for the sake of change."

Occasionally, this means incorporating new technology and engaging fans of the sport in new ways.

"We definitely want the younger group to include us on their bucket list," Lewis says of the importance of reinterpreting the tournament's traditions. "That is an important part of the narrative of Wimbledon."

———

As memorable as updates such as the retractable roof are to Wimbledon's devoted followers, it's the traditions that don't change—for example, the devotion to playing on grass—that are most familiar to casual observers of the tournament. Unique among the four Grand Slams, Wimbledon remains devoted to "lawn tennis" long after others have switched to less expensive surfaces such as concrete and clay. Why stick with grass? Grass courts have their own unique speed and require players to exercise skills differ-

ent from those needed for more consistent surfaces. They also have a limited growing season in most climates, so time, access, and acumen come at a premium. Perhaps because of this, a renewed appreciation for grass courts has led to the recent creation of other professional grass court tournaments besides Wimbledon. Since 2015, professional grass tournaments have been created in Germany, Turkey, and Spain.

"Traditions are an important part of Wimbledon and something to which we give much thought," Lewis stresses. "What are the good traditions that we must keep and value, and what are the traditions that have run their course and perhaps need to move on?"

Wimbledon isn't likely to move on from grass any time soon. The same goes for all-white clothing, another famous tradition that Wimbledon has no plans to change. By requiring players to wear all white, the tournament challenges them to distinguish themselves by the quality of their play, not the clothes they wear.

"We have tightened, not loosened, the rules on white clothing," Lewis says. "When you see a photo of a tennis player playing on a Wimbledon court—due to the lack of sponsorship signage, the grass courts, and the white clothing—it's very identifiable. It can be nowhere else. It can only be Wimbledon."

> "We are ambitious about being successful, moving forward and never resting on our laurels. We won't take things for granted or be complacent."

Other time-honored customs—including the absence of advertising on Centre Court and

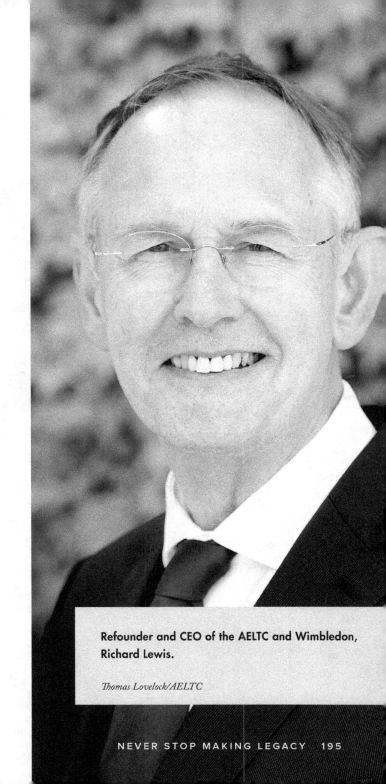

Refounder and CEO of the AELTC and Wimbledon, Richard Lewis.

Thomas Lovelock/AELTC

Ball boys and ball girls at Wimbledon. "We value continuity and tradition here at Wimbledon," says Lewis. "We don't make change, physical or cultural, without serious consideration. It's never change for the sake of change."

Joel Marklund /AELTC

the opening of each match without player introductions, music, or fanfare—remain because they keep the focus on the sport.

"You don't need to introduce these people," Lewis explains. "Spectators, all 15,000 of them, know who they are."

Finally, though not quite as black and white as its dress code, Wimbledon's adherence to proper etiquette—required of spectators and players alike—is also well known in the world of tennis. Though Lewis admits that maintaining proper etiquette among players and fans can be difficult (reconciling formality with fun is something of a moving target), it's all in the name of enjoyment of the sport.

Through it all, Wimbledon holds to its principle of cultivating and sharing the sport with its advocates, annually setting aside some 1,500 show court and several thousand grounds pass tickets for the devoted fans who line up each morning in "the Queue." Despite Wimbledon's reputation as a prestigious tournament, the tradition means that anyone who is passionate about tennis has a chance to attend.

"Ultimately, the driving force is to be the best; to represent the pinnacle of the sport of tennis," says Lewis. "For those of us who work here, we recognize that we have inherited something special, and we aim to continue it. We are ambitious about being successful, moving forward, and never resting on our laurels. We won't take things for granted or be complacent."

By perpetually letting the past inform the present, Wimbledon not only has survived but is thriving as the purest expression of the sport that tennis has to offer. Key to that success is the artful curation of Wimbledon's traditions, which are given careful consideration each year. As a result of its dedication to representing the pinnacle of the sport, Wimbledon is always refining and improving, making meaningful changes to ensure that its legacy in the making continues perpetually in the spirit in which it has been intended since 1877.

In building your modern legacy, how could you keep tradition from becoming too traditional?

Modern legacy brands distinguish between traditions worth maintaining and traditional traits that must evolve. To tell the difference, ask yourself what is essential to your brand and what gets in the way as times and technology change. If you don't examine your traditions and traditional traits, you may hold on to stale expressions out of habit or, worse, leave treasured aspects of the brand behind.

In its quest to embody the pinnacle of the sport, Wimbledon walks the line between traditions and innovations, perpetually vetting new ideas against the brand's enduring ambition. Some traditions remain, such as grass courts, all-white attire, and the lack of fanfare, whereas others have evolved as the times have changed, such as the way the organization uses technology to share its love of tennis with new generations. Ultimately, every decision is made in the interest of the sport, not for the sake of custom or change alone.

Do you understand your brand's traditions and how to keep them from becoming traditional? Rather than repeating the past or renouncing it, perpetually driven leaders and brands build modern legacies by bridging the past, the present, and the future. How will your long-term personal ambition stay vital to new generations as times change? The key here is to ask yourself why your ambition will remain relevant to others today, tomorrow, and every day afterward. Legacies in the making will always benefit from traditions. Being perpetual means ensuring that those traditions never become too traditional.

As part of Wimbledon's commitment to continuous improvement, a retractable roof was installed on Centre Court in 2009. No. 1 Court will gain a similar structure in 2019.

Thomas Lovelock/AELTC

1 **Don't Just Have a Plan, Stick with It**
THE TORONTO MAPLE LEAFS
Established 1917

2 **Let the Past Inform the Present**
THE CHAMPIONSHIPS, WIMBLEDON
Established 1877

3 # Transcend Generations

TAYLOR GUITARS

Established 1974

TODAY, TAYLOR GUITARS is the number one American manufacturer of acoustic guitars, but for decades the brand was known as an upstart in an industry of established icons.[12] The turning point was back in the early 1990s. After nearly a decade of synthesizers and hair-metal bands in the 1980s, musicians were powering down their amplifiers and returning to the warmth and intimacy of the acoustic guitar. Luckily for Taylor Guitars, acoustic had been the brand's specialty since it was founded in 1974.

Inspired by hit series such as *MTV Unplugged*, which featured artists such as Eric Clapton and Nirvana playing acoustic instruments, the early 1990s gave rise to a new generation of guitar players eager to learn. Meanwhile, prime-time programs such as *The Wonder Years*, with its nostalgia for the songs of the 1960s, were drawing baby boomers back to the guitar for the first time in years. With audiences young and old picking up the acoustic guitar, Taylor Guitars' cofounders felt a surge in the marketplace.

"Things started taking off," recalls Kurt Listug, who cofounded the brand with Bob Taylor. "You started hearing acoustic guitar making a comeback on commercials and in soundtracks."

For years, Listug and Taylor had slowly grown their business from a small San Diego shop into a company with national distribution. Taylor designed the guitars, and Listug went from store to store selling them.

When sales picked up across the category, Listug started looking for ways to create a distinctive brand identity compared with its established competitors: better-known brands that included Gibson, Fender, and C.F. Martin & Co. Though his competitors spoke about products or features, he knew the real reasons people loved their Taylors— playing, sharing, and enjoying guitars. In other words, feelings, not features.

It made sense. In Taylor Guitars' case, the cofounders personally loved building and playing guitars. They had a passion for the materials, resonance, and playability of the instrument. Inspired by this insight, the cofounders set out to distinguish their brand by expressing their values to customers who shared them.

Cofounder Kurt Listug, Taylor Guitars.

Image courtesy of Taylor Guitars

They started with the brand's passion for tonewoods, the increasingly scarce species of woods that make the best guitars. "Other guitar brands conventionally focused on celebrity artist endorsements or features," Listug says. "We built a brand that at first showed a less conventional reverence for the trees that brought our guitars and players to life."

Over time, the cofounders' personal ambition to work with innovative designs and rare materials, crafting playable guitars by hand, has set Taylor Guitars apart as a passion-oriented brand that puts musicality before profit.

Each step of the way, sales have followed. In the early 1990s, when acoustic guitars began making a comeback, Taylor Guitars was generating just about $2 million in annual revenue. "From the early 1990s until the early 2000s, we grew to earning more than $50 million a year," Listug recalls. "Over the last several years, we have grown to earning even more than $100 million."

Along the way, Taylor Guitars' cofounders learned a poignant lesson in building their modern legacy: Although people can't transcend generations, their ambitions can. And when those ambitions are passed forward from generation to generation, legacies in the making become perpetual.

———————————

Being perpetual, however, is not the same as being permanent. Perpetual thinking is more fluid than rigid, more like a philosophy than a code or a rule book. As a flexible mindset, perpetual thinking is born out of ambition, adopted and evolved by those who follow, and forever finding new expressions in the now. In Taylor Guitars' case, the cofounders have incorporated their passions into everything they do, from marketing and manufacturing to their supply chain and succession planning. As a result, the heart and soul of the brand they built is living on through the next generation of musicians.

Notably, the company didn't become the leading acoustic guitar brand by trading on its reputation for craftsmanship to crank out high-volume, low-quality products. From the beginning, the brand has stayed true to its belief in making instruments people love to play. Bob Taylor's irreverent attitude toward building and fixing guitars has been the key, says Listug. Early in their partnership, Listug recalls watching Taylor fix a friend's acoustic Guild. Rather than repair it the traditional way, Taylor took a saw to the neck.

> *"As a matter of business routine, Bob and I always like to ask ourselves, 'In 10 years' time, will we be glad that we made each decision?'"*

An early photo of Kurt Listug, cofounder of Taylor Guitars, combining a passion for craft and playability in the company's shop.

Image courtesy of Taylor Guitars

"I remember saying, 'You can't hack away on a guitar like that,'" Listug says. "And Bob said, 'It is the most direct way to fix it.' It made sense to him. It is not that he didn't honor the old ways; it is that the guitar needed the neck angle adjusted, and he required a better way to do it and to put it back together."

Over the years, Listug and Taylor have maintained this innovative approach to everything the brand does, from the way they source materials to the way the guitars are crafted and sold.

"In Bob's way of thinking, the old solutions were a function of the tools that were made available years ago," explains Listug. "And he did not want to limit himself based on the tools that were available a long time ago if he could wind up making a better-playing instrument for today's players."

Driven by a passion to innovate and produce a better instrument, Listug and Taylor were also innovative in the way they ran their business, becoming early adopters of lean manufacturing methods,

opening their own distribution network in Europe to sell directly to retailers and better control their brand, and even acquiring their own ebony supply source to make the notoriously wasteful process of sourcing ebony sustainable. Each of those initiatives grew out of the brand's core belief in making the kinds of guitars the cofounders themselves love to play.

"Taylor Guitars is known for playability," says Listug. "Perfecting playability is something that Bob has worked on forever."

As Taylor Guitars' cofounders approach retirement, they are taking proactive steps to ensure that their modern legacy lives on for generations to come.

"As a matter of business routine, Bob and I always like to ask ourselves, 'In 10 years' time, will we be glad that we made each decision?'" says Listug. "If the answer is yes, that usually means making the kind of investment in personal energy and capital today because we know that down the road the business will be better off. Even if a long-term decision requires us to go outside of our comfort zone, if it's for the sustained

> *"Find something where you're going to feel rewarded by the work, not just the successes."*

success of the business, we'll do it. We've grown very comfortable with the idea of going outside of our comfort zone."

Like Taylor Guitars' cofounders, modern legacy builders who focus on paying their passions forward to future generations before paying profits back to shareholders have a better chance of doing both in the long run. This is perpetual thinking. Akin to planting a tree with no expectation of ever enjoying its shade, the cofounders of Taylor Guitars are investing in a future they can pass forward to the next generation. When Listug and Taylor began considering who would succeed them in leading their brand, they vetted their potential successors through the lens of their long-term personal ambition: a passion for building and playing guitars.

"When we look at most other companies that make a quality product, leadership has often been passed to sales, marketing, and finance people," says Listug. "Even though these great companies were started by an inventor, a tinkerer, a guitar maker, their viewpoint eventually tends to be driven by the idea of making more of what they already sell. They make and sell more of their old legacy products. We never want creativity and manufacturing to take a backseat to sales, marketing, and finance."

To ensure that Taylor Guitars continues to be a passion-oriented brand after they retire, Listug and Taylor chose a successor who shared their curiosity and love for guitar playing.

"Bob wanted somebody who could take the mantle of leadership in creating new instru-

ments to help carry Taylor Guitars into the future. Bob handpicked Andy Powers, now our master luthier—our master builder. He's been with us for five years and is only in his midthirties. Andy can carry this brand into the future. When he is in his fifties, it will be his responsibility to find the next person to mentor, as his protégé, to help carry Taylor Guitars into the future."

If Taylor Guitars' cofounders are right, their legacy in the making will transcend generations, living on through those who share their passions. For the time being, those passions are alive and well. Even as they begin to step back and allow others to guide their brand, their long-term personal ambition continues to resonate perpetually with those who follow.

"Find something that you're really passionate about, that you believe in, that you'll keep at no matter what," Listug advises. "Find something where you're going to feel rewarded by the work, not just the successes. No matter what you do, there are going to be really hard times, so make sure you're working at something that you care about more than anything in order to compel you to keep going on your journey."

In building your modern legacy, how will you feel about today's decisions 10 years from now?

Nearsighted brand leaders lose their perpetual nature because they lose sight of what inspired them in the first place and become fixated on short-term measures of success. That's why many of Taylor Guitars' competitors, rather than innovating, crank out the same familiar models year after year. But relying on past success alone is never the way forward.

To operate in the short term without losing sight of their long-term ambitions, the cofounders of Taylor Guitars instill their short-term decisions with long-term thinking. Before making any important decision, they ask themselves how they will feel about their choice in 10 years.

How would your choices be different if you did the same thing? Would looking through a long-term lens make short-term goals seem less significant? Would long-term ambitions take on new meaning? By drawing back the lens and making today's decisions in service of tomorrow, you may find that you are more comfortable leaving your short-term comfort zone.

Taylor Guitars' innovative design approach is reflected in The Academy Series, a line of guitars that aims to inspire the next generation of guitar players by being easier and more rewarding to play.

Image courtesy of Taylor Guitars

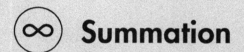 **Summation**

The aspiration to build a brand that lives in perpetuity is perhaps the highest ideal of any modern legacy builder. It requires an appreciation for the past, present, and future. It requires a passion worthy of passing forward. And it requires a lot of skill—and, sometimes, even a little luck. Those who aspire to be perpetually iconic, such as the Toronto Maple Leafs, The Championships, Wimbledon, and Taylor Guitars, integrate their long-term ambitions into their daily practices and find creative ways to ensure that their passions stay vital. In this way, each is making legacy every day.

A perpetual mindset begins with forming a plan and having the stomach to stick with it. This is what Brendan Shanahan and the Toronto Maple Leafs are aspiring to do in the NHL. Step by step, shot by shot, the Leafs are rebuilding their team from the front office down and from the bench up. Each person, from Shanahan and the head coach to the up-and-coming players on the Leafs' farm team, shares in the responsibility for sticking with the plan to help build the next championship era in Toronto.

Once the plan is in action, thinking perpetually means keeping in touch with where you came from while also looking ahead, neither strictly repeating nor reviling the past. Few brands demonstrate this technique as dynamically and diligently as The Championships, Wimbledon, which celebrates its past while simultaneously looking for new ways to express its timeless reverence for the sport of tennis in the modern age. Whereas more and more of today's leaders prefer the ease and speed of cutting free of the past, modern legacy builders such as Richard Lewis at Wimbledon find ways to let the past inform the present.

Finally (though, of course, nothing perpetual is ever final), thinking perpetually means animating without end—forever working to build a modern legacy without a finish line. This is how Taylor Guitars is transcending generations. By passing personal passions forward to others who share them, cofounders Kurt Listug and Bob Taylor are finding a way to ensure that their legacy in the making plays on.

As each of the brands and leaders in this chapter illustrates, a perpetual modern legacy is a personal pursuit that takes shape each day through discrete acts and behaviors as well as a shared pursuit that transcends the individual. In each case, it's the ambitions that drive them onward.

THE LEGACY BUILDER'S
BALANCE SHEET

A Measure For Forever

Early in our work at The Legacy Lab, we conducted research with United Kingdom–based semiotics expert Dr. Alex Gordon to investigate the meaning of the word *legacy*. Dr. Gordon explored two definitions. On the one hand, there was traditional legacy, or "legacy as gifting," such as a bequest in a will, especially of money or other personal property. On the other hand, there was a more modern future-facing approach to legacy—"legacy as transmission"—meaning an idea or a value from an ancestor or predecessor that is perpetually reexpressed. Legacies based on gifting alone risk becoming stuck in the past. Legacies that live on through transmission evolve with each new generation.

Under the leadership of longtime editor David Remnick, *The New Yorker* is an iconic example of a storied brand that has deftly handled both gifting (things that are handed down) and transmission (things that change as they are passed forward). Over time, brands need to either evolve or eliminate ideas from their past while simultaneously finding new ways to transmit the brand forward. Now celebrating its ninety-third year as a magazine, *The New Yorker* also produces a website, live events, festivals, podcasts, a national radio show, various apps, and even an interactive augmented reality feature. Other examples of transmission include the magazine's signature font, which has evolved over the years, and the brand's monocled mascot, Eustace Tilley, the subject of a series of artistic reinterpretations throughout the decades.

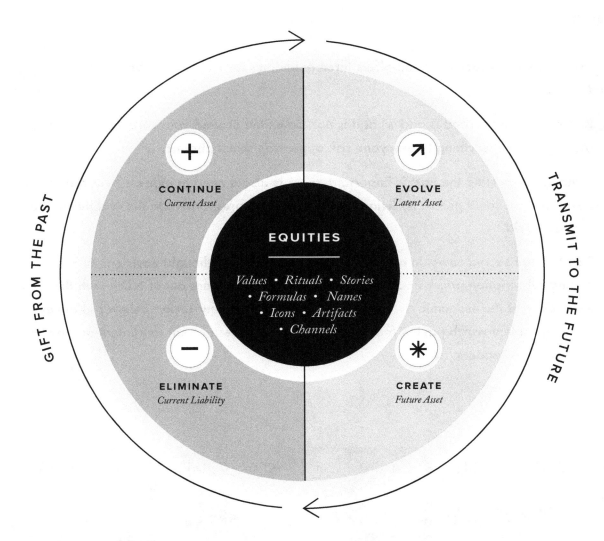

Go Back to the Future

The Perpetual Ledger (above) ensures traditions don't become overly traditional by distinguishing between equities gifted from the past (those you may continue or eliminate) and equities resulting from transmission (those you may create or evolve). After nearly a century in print, *The New Yorker* cultivates a deep portfolio of equities, forever gifting and transmitting aspects of its identity to ensure that its brand remains vital. Actively manage your brand's equities by perpetually asking whether they should be evolved, created, eliminated, or continued.

Source: The Legacy Lab

The New Yorker's leadership team offers three guidelines for transmitting your brand's modern legacy:

1. Know what your brand is and what it is not. Be united around your core values. Brands that try to be everything to everyone risk appearing schizophrenic.

2. Although respecting the past is important, there is also a need to express the brand in the now. Brands cannot persist by living in ivory towers, unresponsive to the realities of the outside world.

3. Don't accept sacred cows. In a world of free content, many thought decisions such as raising subscription prices and charging for online access were out of touch with the times. Regardless of the economic circumstances, however, *The New Yorker* believes in always creating content worth paying for. Because the brand doesn't treat its content as frivolous, neither do its readers.

The iconic face of *The New Yorker*. While the brand's media platforms continue to evolve, its most resonant features persist.

Images courtesy of The New Yorker

Looking at your brand's equities through the lens of gifting and transmission, ask yourself if it's time to evolve, create, eliminate, or continue. Whereas conventional ledgers, which episodically measure conventional assets, aren't dynamic enough for this task, The Legacy Lab's Perpetual Ledger on page 213 is capable of continuously taking both past and future into account.

Examine which of your equities are fixed (giftable, unchanging) and which are flexible (transmittable though rooted in the original spirit). Keep *The New Yorker*'s advice in mind: Avoid schizophrenia, ivory towers, and sacred cows. Instead, stay focused on the core elements of each equity, asking what needs to evolve, what can stay the same, and what should simply go away, creating room for new expressions. By regularly distinguishing between static gifts and dynamic transmissions, you can better track when it's time to evolve, create, eliminate, or continue.

Brands that don't reexamine their equities continually concretize their traditional legacies. Brands that keep a Perpetual Ledger cycle new life into their modern legacies every day.

The Beginning of Your Legacy in the Making

BACK IN 2012, when The Legacy Lab began researching the topic of brand building in the modern era, we started where you might expect: studying pioneering brands. We took a global perspective, researching companies young and old across a wide swath of industries—from technology, hospitality, and sports to philanthropy, consumer packaged goods, and entertainment. In every instance, no matter how iconic the brand, we found that it is the leaders behind the brands—those individuals inspired by long-term personal ambitions—who are building *modern* legacies every day. That is why this isn't just a book about successful brands. At its heart, it is about the rare visionary leaders at the helm of those brands and the ambitions that carry them forward.

In recent years, many of the world's best-known companies have lost their way because their leaders have fallen victim to false dilemmas: Is the best business strategy to guard the past or disregard it? Is legacy a good thing or a bad thing? In today's short-term-obsessed world, most leaders think they have to choose one road or the other. Threatened by change, they choose between fight and flight—clinging to the past or abandoning the old in favor of the now. Focused only on the near term, they make shortsighted decisions. The leaders who accept these false dilemmas ultimately write the endings to their own stories, closing the book on the brands they lead.

Enduring success is not about pitting the past against the future. For lasting brands, the answer lies not in choosing sides but in reconciling them. By bringing the past forward and writing history every day, modern legacy builders can act quickly to create long-term brands that stand out in today's short-term world. This is why, now more than ever, the modern legacy mindset is so valuable: Those who can't act fast don't last long.

In a transparent, on-demand world, markets evolve rapidly. There is less time for deliberating, for board meetings, focus groups, competitive audits, and the like. Dynamic conditions call for leaders who can act decisively, quickly making today's choices in service of tomorrow. Because the modern legacy builders profiled in this book know where they came from and where they aim to be tomorrow, they can respond to today's challenges much faster than can brands that are distracted by every short-term objective. Informed by the past and drawn by the future, these leaders are forever forging legacies in the making.

Unfortunately, modern legacy is still scarce. The counterintuitive logic of the modern legacy mindset is lost on most of today's leaders and brands. In a chaotic, unpredictable era in which business increasingly is characterized by nearsighted decision-making, short-termism is spreading unchecked through business and culture. Not only are enduring brands becoming increasingly rare, the average tenure of business leaders and their brands is shrinking rapidly. Short-termism is a race to the bottom that no one can win.

The way you respond to the constant fluctuations of this short-term world—how you navigate through the daily, weekly, and quarterly distractions—will shape your brand in the long term. You can try to resist change by clinging tightly to the past. You can allow yourself to be swept up in change, rejecting the past entirely. Or you can set your sights on the horizon by using the modern legacy mindset to navigate through whatever this short-term world throws at you.

Now is the time to begin building your modern legacy.

A New Worldview

In this economy of long-term scarcity, leaders with the modern legacy mindset not only are distinguishing themselves from their competitors, they've become touchstones of business, culture, and community. Because they stand for something, consumers gravitate to their cause. Because they lead the way forward, their influence on competitors is gaining momentum. Because they find ways to stay vital, they endure and thrive where others falter. Today, those with the modern legacy mindset are transforming the way strong brands are built in five key ways:

1. From Institutional to Personal

Nearsighted brand leaders buy in to management systems and institutional processes with the goal of following market trends. Leaders with the modern legacy mindset invest in individuals who are seeking to make a meaningful contribution, beginning with their own long-term personal ambitions.

2. From Attitudinal to Behavioral

Nearsighted brand leaders imagine their brands first from the outside in, believing that attitude—what they say and how they posture—matters most. Leaders with the modern legacy mindset build from the inside out in accordance with beliefs that drive behaviors because actions matter more than words alone.

3. From Commanding to Influential

Nearsighted brand leaders hoard information and tell customers what to do, striving for category dominance and sales superiority. Leaders with the modern legacy mindset consider their social influence and invite customers to help tell their story because sales follow saliency.

4. From Orthodox to Unconventional

Nearsighted brand leaders focus on mastering rules (e.g., business is about making profits) and take conventional wisdom for granted (e.g., there are no profits in altruism)—all in the interest of maintaining the status quo. Leaders with the modern legacy mindset forge extraordinary and lasting change by breaking rules, including reconciling paradoxes (e.g., business can make money *and* be a force for good).

5. From Episodic to Perpetual

Nearsighted brand leaders tend to grow stale by repeating the past or to lose their identity by renouncing it. Leaders with the modern legacy mindset find a new way, cultivating enduring significance by bringing the past forward and reinvigorating their brands each day.

Legacy in the Making is our wake-up call for all the short-term thinkers out there—a reminder of the consequences of groupthink and mass myopia. It's a clarion call for a new way to build lasting brands. If you find yourself stuck in the short-term spin cycle, you now have a compass to help you navigate your way out. Let the stories in this book show you the way. The leaders celebrated here stand out because they love what they do, often dedicating their entire lives to making a difference.

From Amazon to Zuckerberg, every modern legacy has to start somewhere. For every global icon near the peak of his or her career, such as Richard Branson and Mark Cuban, The Legacy Lab continues to turn up other visionaries on their way up the mountain. Some, like many of the leaders featured in these pages, are partway there. Still other Legacy Lab interviewees are earlier in the climb. There's Tiffany Pham, the founder and CEO of Mogul, an award-winning media platform that allows women to connect, share information, and access knowledge from one another with the goal of enabling learning and collaboration all over the world. There's Scott Harrison, the founder and CEO of charity: water, a non-profit organization striving to bring clean and safe drinking water to people in developing nations. There's Debbie Sterling, the founder and CEO of GoldieBlox, a multimedia brand "disrupting the pink aisle in toy stores" with STEM-based toys, games, and entertainment that challenge gender stereotypes.

Modern legacy builders like these don't live to work or work to live; they bring their whole selves to everything they do. All of us benefit as they succeed at their ambitions.

Write Your Own Story Every Day

Whether you are running your own company, leading an established brand, or aspiring to do either one, our call to action is this: Start making a meaningful contribution today.

Dream big. Set an audacious ambition and stick with it. Inspire those around you and incorporate your ambition into your life and work. Don't leave your job at the office or limit your living to evenings and weekends. Leverage your personal ambitions to live a life of significance, making legacy every day. In a world caught up in short-term thinking, author your own long-term story. With enduring ambition, you can do what few others are willing or able to do—create something worthwhile that others will want to be a part of and that will flourish for generations to come.

No matter what the industry, the age of the brand, or the competitive challenges, the wellspring of all lasting brands is long-term personal ambition. All the other transformative principles in the modern legacy mindset, though equally important, flow from there.

When you get spun around by short-term circumstances, return to the guidance in these pages to orient yourself. When you lose your way, the lessons we have distilled from years of research are all here to help guide you onward.

When we say you should write your own story, we mean just that. Be the author of your own modern legacy. The stories here aren't meant to be copied literally. Instead, consider this book a living text. *Legacy in the Making* is a guide—a book of modern business philosophy and an inspiration to help you achieve your long-term personal ambition.

Rather than replicating what's been done, we hope this book inspires you to imagine and create brands, products, services, and solutions that do not yet exist. In the words of John Steinbeck, "Man, unlike anything organic or inorganic in the universe, grows beyond his work, walks up the stairs of his concepts, emerges ahead of his accomplishments."[1] When you are guided by your long-term personal ambition, the potential of your modern legacy is limitless.

We hope this book also inspires you to write the chapters we have not yet written. The short-term world needs more farsighted leaders. As we write this, our colleagues at The Legacy Lab are searching the world for inspiring legacies in the making. We know a few readers will put this book down and forget it. We know others will try a few ideas and quit. Some, however, will apply these lessons and make a lasting difference.

With these closing words, we call on you to begin building a modern legacy that is worth celebrating. The next chapter, the one about you and your ambition, is one you must write yourself. Create something of enduring substance and significance. Chart your course on the basis of your own ambition. Drive positive change. Add your story to the ones in these pages.

Just as we began with an ending—the end of legacy as we know it—*Legacy in the Making* ends at the beginning: the beginning of your own modern legacy. From here, you must decide whether to write history every day or simply read from it. How you start and whether you can build a brand that makes a long-term difference in this short-term world begins with your personal ambition. The only person who can write that story is you.

Acknowledgments

Howard Schultz, executive chairman and former CEO of Starbucks Coffee Co., often is quoted as saying, "When you're surrounded by people who share a passionate commitment around a common purpose, anything is possible."[1] The necessity of surrounding yourself with others who believe the way you do in the pursuit of bringing something meaningful to life was brought to the fore for us, as authors, in writing *Legacy in the Making*. This book would not have been possible without the dedicated team of contributors and supporters, all those believers and coauthors who gave so much of themselves in the spirit of helping to move our work forward.

For those who love a good origin story, the concept for this book was born in early June 2016, when some of the founding members of The Legacy Lab gathered around a conference room table to organize key themes and ideas from research that was already years in the making: Adrian Barrow, Chris Graves, Heather Hogan, and Lauren Mabuni. Our siren call was to honor the stories and lessons shared with us by leaders and to spark future stories and lessons by passing our accumulated knowledge forward. For the next 18 months—over many long days, nights, and weekends—Adrian, Chris, Heather, and Lauren each contributed countless hours researching, thinking, and ideating on the book to help shape the way the business leaders of today and tomorrow would look at the subject of legacy anew.

Over the course of researching and writing, a critical core of extended team members contributed boundless energy, creativity, and smarts in support of *Legacy in the Making*. Ami Barber, Alison Beck, Emily Chidester, Rachel Crain, Chris D'Rozario, Meredith Gruen, Jamie Kerr, Melanie Lee, Nathan Manchester, Howard Moggs, Tera Morris, David Peake, Steve Sapka, Robert Sedlack, Meg Seiler, Nick Vianna, and Helen Zuliani. Each brought unique skills to the team, but it was their selfless approach and above-and-beyond input across many stages of creating this book that made their contributions not only helpful but essential. This team of core supporters treated *Legacy in the Making* as a calling beyond a job, and we couldn't have been more fortunate to have them working at our side.

Although the words in this book tell a lot of the story, the visualization of those words helps reveal even more. The design thinking in *Legacy in the Making* was contributed by Sophia Arriola-Gibson, Brian Doyle, Adrienne Ford, Matt Hartz, Tim Meraz, and the group at Sawdust. More than lending artistry and illustration, all the designers who worked on the book brought conceptual thinking to their submissions, at times motivating the writing to help amplify their concepts rather than the other way around. As the notion of looking at legacy as something that is perpetually unfolding is a newer idea, it took a group of designers with the imagination to see the future and the talent to communicate it clearly for us to succeed.

Significantly, neither The Legacy Lab's body of work nor the *Legacy in the Making* book would be here if not for the continued support of key members of the leadership team at Publicis Groupe's Team One: Julie Michael, Kurt Ritter, and Michael Webb. At a time when many conventional advertising agencies emphasize offering similar services to keep up with the times, Julie, Kurt, and Michael have made a sustained investment in thought leadership, including the study and practice of modern legacy making, to lead the industry forward. For these agency leaders, modern legacy making is more than a new marketing idea; it is also a lifelong commitment to working with brands that seek to make an enduring difference through their work.

From the moment they accepted our proposal, all the way through, to editing and publishing, the team at McGraw-Hill Education championed the premise of *Legacy in the Making*. Donya Dickerson and Cheryl Ringer were the first to review and approve and—along with Pattie Amoroso, Maureen Harper and everyone at McGraw-Hill Education—always treated our subject matter and writing as something with importance. They didn't just buy our book, they bought into our way of looking at legacy as something forever in the making. In turn, we are proud to say that they aren't just our publishing partner but are also part of our team of believers.

Fundamentally, this book is a celebration of leaders—founders, cofounders, and refounders—building brands that are making a long-term impact in a short-term world. The leadership stories we've gathered over many years have made a lasting impression on us as authors, gifts that we aim to pass forward to you, our readers. For all their contributions to our research and writing, we wanted to acknowledge the leaders celebrated in this book who have shared their stories with us: Brent Bushnell, Yvon Chouinard, Deb Dugan, Christopher Gavigan, Craig Hatkoff, Hervé Humler, Chris Kay, Toni Ko, Amy Kurland, Alwyn Hight Kushner, Richard Lewis, Kurt Listug, Ted Molter, Erika Wollam Nichols, Reshma Saujani, Dan Savage, Brendan Shanahan, Mark Templin, François Thibault, Mikaila Ulmer, and Alan Webber. Thank you for building the kinds of brands whose legacies are perpetually inspiring and in the making.

Thank you also to all those key supporters at each of the brands represented in *Legacy in the Making* for providing open access to their organizations and leaders: Arjorie Arong, Jerry Brown, Huw Davies, Marla del Rosario, Maria Diaz, Mike Dunn, Elaine Fintel, Lori Hoffman, Rita Hoffman, Lisa Holladay, Nancy Hubbell, Steve Keogh, Hilary Kinney, Jim Kirlin, Rachel Mandel, Grace Martinez, Monica Michel, Alexandra Miller, Tim O'Brien, Kelly Parisi, Laura Patterson, Johnny Perkins, Brian Pines, Natalie Raabe, Emily Schienvar, Joanne Simons, Christina Simmons, Allison Sitch, Nick Teare, Michael Tripp, D'Andra Ulmer, Theo Ulmer, Mauricio Vergara, Jonathan Yepez, and Annabelle Withers. To bring so many stories to life all in one book took the dedicated support of so many other people who, on top of their daily responsibilities, gave to this book as if it were one of their core responsibilities. These supporters have been with us on each step of the journey from interviewing and writing to fact checking, always helping to make the impossible possible.

Going back to when The Legacy Lab began as a pure academic exploration, before it was called The Legacy Lab or before there was an idea to write a book, there was an entrepreneurial team of bright thinkers and makers who invested in this subject with a real passion: Laura Albers, Rudi Anthony, Leandro Arroyo, Rachel Bensimon, Jennie DuMonde, Ashleigh Edwards, Elaine Evangelista, Lisamarie Gaulin, Jen Grant, Kevin Helms, Shane Herr, Angela Jones, Nikole Knak, Susanna Leighton, Karen Link, Kari Niessink-Takai, Sophie Ozoux, Scholastica Park, Matt Reamer, Rosheila Robles, Alex Sharkey, Kevin Shuster, Julie Smith, Angela Stowers, Mary Toves, Davide Vismara, Mena Xiong, Jacky Yang, Joanna Young, and Yisha Zhang. We would be remiss in recounting the origins of *Legacy in the Making* if we did not acknowledge those who contributed to its foundations. Had it not been for their investment of time and energy, this work would have persisted as an unexamined thesis—a dream and not a reality. There was also an important senior-level leadership team that saw the potential in our research, that invested in our work to help grow it from a pilot into a proper lab: Bill Cochrane, Paul Mareski, and Kevin Roberts. *Legacy in the Making* has roots that go all the way back to those leaders who had the vision to understand the contemporary meaning of legacy in a modern context.

In addition to those who affected this book directly, there was a team that supported and motivated us at various stages in the writing process, among them academic minds, business visionaries, and thought leaders such as Caley Cantrell, Mick Ebeling, Alex Gordon, Lisa Hughes, Adi Ignatius, Joseph Michelli, Adam Morgan, Tiffany Pham, B. Joseph Pine II, Bob Safian, Eric Schurenberg, Brian Sheehan, Simon Sinek, Jim Stengel and Brian Sweeney. Each, in their own way, was able to add a layer of wisdom that inspired us along in pursuit of our ambition to share all that we were learning.

Under the heading of business being personal, the enduring support of our cherished families and close friends also encouraged us to think and write: Sally Yang Miller, Hailey Maya Miller, Herman and Vivan Miller, Allan Miller, Gayle and David Drutz, Leo and Helen Yang, Sharon Kondo, Nada Kabbani, Meija Jacobs, Nicole Diaz, Christopher and Katharine Conley, Olivia and Dan Long, and Charles and Dannica Conley. For an extended period, we poured our hearts into making this book because of how important it is to us to contribute something of significance and to make a lasting impact on the way business is practiced. We are both fortunate to be surrounded by family and friends who believe in us, our ideas, and our work.

Finally, thank you to the many people who gave time, energy, creativity, and support to The Legacy Lab, The Legacy Lab Honors, and *Legacy in the Making*, whose names are not listed here but whose contributions have had a lasting impact on our ongoing work. As Howard Schultz said, with a team of passionate, committed people, anything is possible.

Endnotes

Foreword

[1] Since 1985, Patagonia has pledged 1 percent of its sales to the preservation and restoration of the natural environment as part of the 1% for the Planet initiative.

Introduction

[1] Blockbuster: September 23, 2010; Borders: February 16, 2011; Kodak: January 19, 2012.

[2] Although the Kodak and Blockbuster brands survive in some fashion to this day—Blockbuster, in isolated locations, and Kodak, through a recent foray into cryptocurrency—Borders no longer operates.

[3] U.S. Bureau of Labor Statistics, Business Employment Dynamics, April 28, 2016, https://www.bls.gov/bdm/entrepreneurship/bdm_chart3.htm. Retrieved January 2, 2018.

[4] Bouree Lam, "Where Do Firms Go When They Die?" *The Atlantic*, April 12, 2015, https://www.theatlantic.com/business/archive/2015/04/where-do-firms-go-when-they-die/390249/ (citing Richard Foster, Yale School of Management).

[5] *Ibid.*

[6] "Lifespan of Playgrounds," Superior Recreational Products. https://srpplayground.com/how-long-do-playgrounds-last. *See also* Mark Lawton, "New playgrounds aim high in Lake Bluff," *Chicago Tribune*, August 2, 2016, http://www.chicagotribune.com/suburbs/lake-forest/news/ct-lfr-playgrounds-tl-0804-20160802-story.html.

[7] U.S. Bureau of Labor Statistics, September 22, 2016, https://www.bls.gov/news.release/tenure.nr0.htm. Retrieved January 2, 2018.

[8] "Chief Marketing Officer Average Tenure Drops to 42 Months," Spencer Stuart, March 2017, https://www.spencerstuart.com/research-and-insight/chief-marketing-officer-average-tenure-drops-to-42-months. Retrieved January 2, 2018.

[9] Gallup, Inc., "Gallup Daily: U.S. Employee Engagement," July 31, 2017, http://news.gallup.com/poll/180404/gallup-daily-employee-engagement.aspx. Retrieved January 2, 2018.

[10] Team One is Publicis Groupe's premium and luxury brand agency.

Chapter 1

[1] David Kirkpatrick, *The Facebook Effect: The Inside Story of the Company That Is Connecting the World*, New York: Simon & Schuster, 2011, p. 330.

[2] Matthew J. Belvedere, "We Tried to Buy Facebook for Just $24 Billion, Says Microsoft CEO Steve Ballmer," *CNBC*, October 21, 2016, https://www.cnbc.com/2016/10/21/we-tried-to-buy-facebook-for-just-24-billion-says-ex-microsoft-ceo-steve-ballmer.html.

[3] David Kirkpatrick, "Mark Zuckerberg, Social Revolutionary," *Forbes*, May 16, 2012, https://www.forbes.com/sites/techonomy/2012/05/16/mark-zuckerberg-social-revolutionary/#7b1d523369ac.

[4] Julia Boorstein, "Inside Facebook's Futuristic New Headquarters," *CNBC*, May 22, 2015, https://www.cnbc.com/2015/05/22/inside-facebooks-futuristic-new-headquarters.html.

[5] Alex Heath, "Steve Ballmer Says Microsoft Once Tried to Buy Facebook for $24 Billion," *Business Insider*, October 21, 2016, http://www.businessinsider.com/steve-ballmer-microsoft-tried-to-buy-facebook-for-24-billion-2016-10.

[6] Kristina Zucchi, "Why Facebook Is Banned in China," Investopedia, April 29, 2015, https://www.investopedia.com/articles/investing/042915/why-facebook-banned-china.asp.

[7] Vindu Goel and Nick Wingfield, "Mark Zuckerberg Vows to Donate 99% of His Facebook Shares for Charity," *New York Times*, December 1, 2015, https://www.nytimes.com/2015/12/02/technology/mark-zuckerberg-facebook-charity.html.

[8] Matt Egan, "Facebook and Amazon Hit $500 Billion Milestone," *CNN Money*, July 27, 2017, http://money.cnn.com/2017/07/27/investing/facebook-amazon-500-billion-bezos-zuckerberg/index.html.

[9] *Forbes*, https://www.forbes.com/profile/mark-zuckerberg/. Retrieved January 16, 2018.

[10] "The Top 20 Valuable Facebook Statistics – Updated November 2017," *Zephoria*, https://zephoria.com/top-15-valuable-facebook-statistics/.

[11] Daisuke Wakabayashi, "Microsoft Beats Google to Facebook Stake," *Reuters*, October 24, 2007, https://www.reuters.com/article/us-facebook/microsoft-beats-google-to-facebook-stake-idUSN2424560420071024.

[12] Mark Zuckerberg, *Facebook.com*, June 27, 2017.

[13] United States Census Bureau, U.S. and World Population Clock, https://www.census.gov/popclock/. Retrieved January 2, 2018.

[14] As B. C. Forbes, founder of *Forbes* magazine, put it, "Business was originated to produce happiness, not to pile up millions."

[15] Geoff Colvin, "Crisis Chief: AmEx's Chenault," *Fortune*, October 15, 2009, http://archive.fortune.com/2009/10/14/news/companies/american_express_chenault.fortune/index.htm.

[16] Richard Lezin Jones, "Amex Agrees to Reoccupy Damaged Site Downtown," *New York Times*, December 1, 2001, http://www.nytimes.com/2001/12/01/nyregion/amex-agrees-to-reoccupy-damaged-site-downtown.html.

[17] Meghan Giannotta, "Tribeca Film Festival Secrets: Little-Known Facts about Robert De Niro's Annual NYC Event," *am New York*, April 12, 2016, https://www.amny.com/secrets-of-new-york/tribeca-film-festival-secrets-little-known-facts-about-robert-de-niro-s-annual-nyc-event-1.11615029.

[18] Tribeca Film Festival Press Release, "2017 Tribeca Film Festival Announces Attendance and Live Streaming Numbers," May 17, 2017, https://tribecafilm.com/press-center/press-releases/2017-tribeca-film-festival-announces-attendance-and-live-streaming-numbers.

[19] America's Richest Self-Made Women, *Forbes*, June 21, 2016, https://www.forbes.com/self-made-women/.

[20] Clare O'Connor, "Banking on Beauty: How Toni Ko Built NYX Cosmetics into a $500 Million Brand," *Forbes*, June 1, 2016, https://www.forbes.com/sites/clareoconnor/2016/06/01/toni-ko-nyx-cosmetics-loreal-sale-richest-women/#5faa7e207d71.

Chapter 2

[1] Rajen Sanghvi, "39 Quotes from Brian Chesky on Company Culture and Building a Team," *Medium*, October 23, 2014, https://medium.com/how-to-start-a-startup/39-quotes-from-brian-chesky-on-company-culture-and-building-a-team-287573aab3f5.

[2] Brian Chesky, "Don't Fuck Up the Culture," *Medium*, April 20, 2014, https://medium.com/@bchesky/dont-fuck-up-the-culture-597cde9ee9d4.

[3] Sanghvi, "39 Quotes from Brian Chesky."

[4] Chesky, "Don't Fuck Up the Culture."

[5] Leigh Gallagher, "How Airbnb Found a Mission—and a Brand," *Fortune*, December 22, 2016, http://fortune.com/airbnb-travel-mission-brand/.

[6] Katrina Brooker, "Airbnb's Ambitious Second Act Will Take It Way Beyond Couch-Surfing," *Vanity Fair*, November 2016, https://www.vanityfair.com/news/2016/11/airbnb-brian-chesky.

[7] Abha Bhattarai, "Airbnb Hires Eric Holder to Help Company Fight Discrimination," *Washington Post*, July 20, 2016, https://www.washingtonpost.com/news/business/wp/2016/07/20/eric-holder-joins-airbnb-to-help-company-fight-discrimination/.

[8] Alex Fitzpatrick, "Airbnb CEO: 'Bias and Discrimination Have No Place' Here," *Time*, September 8, 2016, http://time.com/4484113/airbnb-ceo-brian-chesky-anti-discrimination-racism/.

[9] Brian Chesky, "An Update on the Airbnb Anti-Discrimination Review," *Airbnb*, July 20, 2016, https://blog.atairbnb.com/an-update-on-the-airbnb-anti-discrimination-review/. Retrieved January 2, 2018.

[10] Belinda Johnson, "Airbnb Welcomes Beth Axelrod as VP of Employee Experience," *Airbnb*, January 13, 2017, https://press.atairbnb.com/welcome-beth-axelrod-2/. Retrieved January 2, 2018.

[11] Leigh Gallagher, "Airbnb's Profits to Top $3 Billion by 2020," *Fortune*, February 15, 2017, http://fortune.com/2017/02/15/airbnb-profits/ (revenue reportedly anticipated by Airbnb in 2017).

[12] Bronwen Clune, "How Airbnb Is Building Its Culture Through Belonging," *Culture Amp*, July 27, 2015, https://blog.cultureamp.com/how-airbnb-is-building-its-culture-through-belonging.

[13] Widely attributed to Dee Hock.

[14] Serena Ng, "Jessica Alba's Honest Co. to Drop Use of Disputed Ingredient," *The Wall Street Journal*, September 30, 2016.

[15] "About NSAI," *NSAI*, https://www.nashvillesongwriters.com/about-nsai.

[16] Official Website of Garth Brooks, http://garthbrooks.com/#garth101 (citing RIAA sales totals). *See also* Stephen L. Betts, "Garth Brooks Surpasses Elvis Presley in Album Sales . . . Again," *Rolling Stone*, January 13, 2105, https://www.rollingstone.com/music/news/garth-brooks-surpasses-elvis-presley-in-album-sales-again-20150113 (citing Beatles sales). Retrieved January 2, 2018.

[17] The Legacy Lab. Interview with Hervé Humler, 2017. The Ritz-Carlton topped its 2016 score in 2017, tying with JW Marriott for number one. *See* "Growth in Mobile Usage for Hotel Stays Presents Opportunity, Challenge for Hoteliers, J.D. Power Finds," *J.D. Power*, http://www.jdpower.com/press-releases/jd-power-2017-north-america-hotel-guest-satisfaction-index-study.

[18] William Taylor, "A Quick History of *Fast Company*," https://williamctaylor.com/fast-company/.

Chapter 3

[1] Jason Fell, "Mark Cuban: Three Tips for Startups," *Entrepreneur*, March 15, 2011, https://www.entrepreneur.com/article/219324.

[2] Interview with Mark Cuban, "Masters in Business: Dallas Mavericks Mark Cuban," interview by Barry Ritholtz, *Bloomberg View*, Bloomberg Radio, November 8, 2014, https://soundcloud.com/bloombergview/masters-in-business-dallas.

[3] Kara Swisher and Evan Ramstad, "Yahoo! to Announce Acquisition of Broadcast.com for $5.7 Billion," *Wall Street Journal*, April 1, 1999, https://www.wsj.com/articles/SB922916873273123235.

[4] Ritholtz, "Masters in Business: Dallas Mavericks Mark Cuban." *See also* "The Business of Basketball," *Forbes*, https://www.forbes.com/teams/dallas-mavericks/.

[5] "The World's Billionaires," *Forbes*, https://www.forbes.com/billionaires/.

[6] Hyatt Corporation, "Stay for Good with (ANDAZ)^RED at Andaz West Hollywood," https://andaz.hyatt.com/en/andaz/inspiration.html.

[7] "Twitter Turns Red for World Aids Day," *The Telegraph*, December 1, 2009, http://www.telegraph.co.uk/technology/twitter/6700836/Twitter-turns-red-for-World-Aids-Day.html.

[8] San Diego Zoo Global is a not-for-profit organization headquartered in San Diego that operates the San Diego Zoo, the San Diego Zoo Safari Park, the San Diego Zoo Institute for Conservation Research, and the San Diego Zoo Global Wildlife Conservancy.

[9] Florence Christman, *The Romance of Balboa Park*, 4th ed., San Diego: San Diego Historical Society, 1985.

[10] "Remembering Billy Lucas, the Boy Whose Suicide Inspired a Movement," *LGBTQ Nation*, September 9, 2013, https://www.lgbtqnation.com/2013/09/remembering-billy-lucas-the-boy-whose-suicide-inspired-a-movement/.

[11] "The 30 Most Influential Teens of 2017," *Time*, November 3, 2017, http://time.com/5003930/most-influential-teens-2017/.

[12] National Retail Foundation, 2017, https://gala.nrf.com/alumni. Retrieved October 17, 2017.

Chapter 4

[1] Interview with Jeff Bezos, "Amazon.com CEO Jeffrey Bezos Shares His Business Strategy with Stern Alumni and Students," interview by Kevin Maney, *Conde Nast Portfolio C-Circuit* (transcript published in *Wired*, May 22, 2008).

[2] Luisa Yanez, "Jeff Bezos: A Rocket Launched from Miami's Palmetto High," *Miami Herald*, August 5, 2013, http://www.miamiherald.com/news/local/community/miami-dade/article1953866.html.

[3] Jillian D'Onfro and Eugene Kim, "The Life and Awesomeness of Amazon Founder and CEO Jeff Bezos," *Business Insider*, February 11, 2016, http://www.businessinsider.com/the-life-of-amazon-founder-ceo-jeff-bezos-2014-7.

[4] Matt Egan, "Facebook and Amazon Hit $500 Billion Milestone," *CNN Money*, July 27, 2017, http://money.cnn.com/2017/07/27/investing/facebook-amazon-500-billion-bezos-zuckerberg/index.html.

[5] Lauren Gensler, "The World's Largest Retailers 2017: Amazon & Alibaba Are Closing in on Wal-Mart," *Forbes*, May 24, 2017, https://www.forbes.com/sites/laurengensler/2017/05/24/the-worlds-largest-retailers-2017-walmart-cvs-amazon/#5aa00bb720b5.

[6] Yanez, "Jeff Bezos: A Rocket Launched from Miami's Palmetto High."

[7] Brett Molina, "Four of the Wildest Ideas from Amazon's Jeff Bezos," *USA Today*, April 27, 2017, https://www.usatoday.com/story/tech/talkingtech/2017/04/27/jeff-bezos-amazon-bold-ideas/100969258/.

[8] *See, e.g.*, Jeff Bezos, "Letter to Amazon Shareholders," *Amazon*, April 12, 2017, https://www.amazon.com/p/feature/z6o9g6sysxur57t. Retrieved January 2, 2018.

[9] Seth Fiegerman, "Amazon now has more than 500,000 employees," *CNN*, October 26, 2017, http://money.cnn.com/2017/10/26/technology/business/amazon-earnings/index.html.

[10] Shana Lebowitz, "Jeff Bezos Uses a Simple Exercise to Decide Which Risks Are Worth Taking," *Business Insider*, June 16, 2017, http://www.businessinsider.com/jeff-bezos-amazon-decides-on-risks-2017-6. *See also* Tim Mullaney, "5 Key Business Lessons from Amazon's Jeff Bezos," *CNBC*, January 12, 2017, https://www.cnbc.com/2016/05/13/5-key-business-lessons-from-amazons-jeff-bezos.html.

[11] John Furrier, "After Winning Cloud, Amazon Web Services CEO Takes Aim at the Rest of Tech," *Forbes*, November 28, 2016, https://www.forbes.com/sites/siliconangle/2016/11/28/after-winning-cloud-amazon-web-services-ceo-takes-aim-at-the-rest-of-tech/#68d54ec65b84.

[12] Shurnryu Suzuki, *Zen Mind, Beginner's Mind*, Boston: Shambala Publications Inc., 2011, p. 1.

[13] Sidney Frank, "How I Did It: Sidney Frank, Founder, Sidney Frank Importing," interview with Stephanie Clifford, *Inc.*, September 1, 2005, https://www.inc.com/magazine/20050901/qa.html.

[14] Renee Montagne, "Bacardi Biography Details The 'Fight For Cuba'," *NPR Morning Edition*, September 8, 2008, https://www.npr.org/templates/story/story.php?storyId=94320922.

[15] *See* 22 C.F.R. §5.22(a)(1) 2016 (emphasis added).

[16] Frank, "How I Did It: Sidney Frank, Founder, Sidney Frank Importing."

[17] Marina Renton, "Ten years in, Sidney Frank legacy endures in scholarship," *The Brown Daily Herald*, September 30, 2014.

[18] Brown University, Sidney E. Frank Scholars, https://www.brown.edu/about/administration/financial-aid/sidney-e-frank-scholars. Retrieved January 2, 2018.

[19] Michael O'Connell, "TV Ratings: Triple Crown Hopes Drive 21 Million to Belmont Stakes," *Hollywood Reporter*, June 8, 2014, https://www.hollywoodreporter.com/live-feed/tv-ratings-triple-crown-hopes-710122.

[20] Toyota Motor Corporation, "For us this was not only a tremendous challenge and a dream to fulfill, but an inevitable decision...," *Toyota Traditions*, July 2003, http://www.toyota-global.com/company/toyota_traditions/innovation/jul_aug_2003.html.

[21] Taiichi Ohno, "Ask 'Why' Five Times About Every Matter," *Toyota Traditions*, March 2006, www.toyota-global.com/company/toyota_traditions/quality/mar_apr_2006.html.

[22] Text of full article available at http://articles.latimes.com/1989-12-05/business/fi-123_1_lexus-ls.

[23] To support Toyota's F1 project, Saatchi & Saatchi, Toyota's longtime advertising agency, formed Team One to create and market the Lexus brand, a relationship that continues to this day.

[24] Chester Dawson, *Lexus: The Relentless Pursuit*, Hoboken, NJ: John Wiley & Sons, 2004, p. 23.

Chapter 5

[1] Richard Branson, *Like a Virgin: Secrets They Won't Teach You at Business School*, New York: Portfolio, 2012, p. 56.

[2] Virgin Group, "About Us," https://www.virgin.com/virgingroup/content/about-us. Retrieved January 2, 2018.

[3] Jason Fell, "10 Ways You Can Be More Like Richard Branson," *Entrepreneur*, May 26, 2015, https://www.entrepreneur.com/slideshow/224672.

[4] Virgin Group, "About Us," https://www.virgin.com/virgingroup/content/about-us. Retrieved January 2, 2018.

[5] Fell, "10 Ways You Can Be More Like Richard Branson."

[6] Kevin Lynch, "Sir Richard Branson's Incredible Treble Makes Guinness World Record 2014 Book," *Guinness World Records*, September 5, 2013, http://www.guinnessworldrecords.com/news/2013/9/sir-richard-branson-incredible-treble-makes-guinness-world-record-2014-book-51036.

[7] Sam Webb, "Richard Branson Reunited with Record-Breaking Superboat 27 Years After It Became the Fastest Ever Vessel to Cross the Atlantic," *Daily Mail*, August 6, 2013, http://www.dailymail.co.uk/news/article-2385549/Richard-Branson-reunited-record-breaking-superboat-27-years-fastest-vessel-cross-Atlantic.html.

[8] Profile of Richard Branson, *Forbes*, December 15, 2017, https://www.forbes.com/profile/richard-branson/.

[9] Richard Branson, "What businesses can learn from breaking records," *Virgin Group*, https://www.virgin.com/richard-branson/what-businesses-can-learn-breaking-records. Retrieved January 2, 2018.

[10] Sarah Lyall, "Centre Court Without Rain? What's Next, Clay?" *New York Times*, June 20, 2009, https://mobile.nytimes.com/2009/06/21/sports/tennis/21roof.html.

[11] The Championships, Wimbledon, Schedule, https://www.wimbledon.com/en_GB/atoz/schedule.html. Retrieved January 2, 2018.

[12] *See, e.g.*, Jefferson Graham, "Meet the Guys Who Build Taylor Swift and Jason Mraz's Guitars," *USA Today*, August 5, 2014, https://www.usatoday.com/story/money/business/2014/08/04/taylor-guitars-poised-for-best-year-ever-for-40th-anniversary/13295397/.

Conclusion

[1] John Steinbeck, *The Grapes of Wrath*, reissue edition, New York: Penguin Classics, 2006, p. 150.

Acknowledgments

[1] Carmine Gallo, "What Starbucks CEO Howard Schultz Taught Me About Communication and Success," *Forbes*, December 19, 2013, https://www.forbes.com/sites/carminegallo/2013/12/19/what-starbucks-ceo-howard-schultz-taught-me-about-communication-and-success/#7f56e98328af.

Index

About the Authors

Mark Miller is the founder of The Legacy Lab, a research and consulting practice, and the chief strategy officer at Team One. Named a Trendsetter and an Agency Innovator by *The Internationalist*, his work in helping global brands drive change has earned awards and recognitions from the Advertising Research Foundation, the American Association of Advertising Agencies, and Effie Worldwide. In addition to his work with The Legacy Lab, readers can learn more about Miller's work on The Global Affluent Tribe (examining global citizens more connected by what they love than by where they live) and The Moonshot Speaker Series (exploring not only the entrepreneurial dreamers, but also the successful doers) at teamone-usa.com.

Miller is a graduate of the Schulich School of Business at York University. Originally from Toronto, Canada, he lives in Los Angeles, California, with his wife, Sally, and their daughter, Hailey. Miller's modern legacy is building and restoring great brands through finding more relevant ways to continue their stories.

Lucas Conley is a writer with The Legacy Lab, the author of *Obsessive Branding Disorder* (one of *Strategy + Business*'s best books of 2008), and coauthor of *The Method Method* (listed as a "top ten" marketing book in 2011 by *Advertising Age*). A former researcher for *The Atlantic* and staff writer for *Fast Company*, he has written for *The Boston Globe*, *ESPN: The Magazine*, *SPIN*, and *The Wall Street Journal Magazine*. A journalist with an eye for stories that change how we see the world, Conley has appeared on The Colbert Report, ABC World News, CNN's BookTV, NPR, and at South by Southwest.

Conley holds a BA in creative writing from the University of Arizona and JD from the University of New Mexico School of Law. Though he resides in Los Angeles, California, between writing projects he lights out for North America's remote and spectacular wildlands. Conley's modern legacy is exploring the human dimension of business through storytelling.

CPSIA information can be obtained
at www.ICGtesting.com
Printed in the USA
BVHW022359140223
658548BV00011B/187

9 781264 948253